HEAD RAMBLES

Richard O'Connor

HEAD RAMBLES

with Ireland's most cantankerous auld fella

MERCIER PRESS
WHAT YOU NEED TO READ

MERCIER PRESS
Cork
www. mercierpress. ie

Trade enquiries to CMD,
55A Spruce Avenue, Stillorgan Industrial Park,
Blackrock, County Dublin

© Richard O'Connor, 2009

ISBN: 978 1 85635 616 9

10 9 8 7 6 5 4 3 2 1
A CIP record for this title is available from the British Library

Back cover illustration courtesy of Kate O'Connor

 Mercier Press receives financial assistance from the Arts Council/An Chomhairle Ealaíon

This book is sold subject to the condition that it shall not, by way of trade or otherwise, be lent, resold, hired out or otherwise circulated without the publisher's prior consent in any form of binding or cover other than that in which it is published and without a similar condition including this condition being imposed on the subsequent purchaser.
  No part of this publication may be reproduced or transmitted in any form or by any means, electronic or mechanical, including photocopying, recording or any information or retrieval system, without the prior permission of the publisher in writing.
  All characters, locations and events in this book are entirely fictional. Any resemblance to any person, living or dead, which may occur inadvertently is completely unintentional.

Printed and bound in the EU.

CONTENTS

Introduction	11
My county council likes me	13
How to survive your first Guinness	14
Answer this one	16
In the dark	18
Not a grump	19
People out there really like me	20
Put your wallet away. I'll get this	21
I've been zeroed	22
Experience desired, but not essential	23
Life from the viewpoint of a goldfish	25
Go kick your balls before I do	27
Holy smoke! Oireachtas Report is funny!	30
Why I hate the Dawn Chorus	31
Please leave a message after the tone ...	32
Does my bum look big in this?	34
On the road to nowhere	36
Take two before going to school	37
Afternoon coffee	39
Oh for the open road	40
Mad Broadband (part 1)	42
Mad Broadband (Part 2)	45
Mad Broadband (Part 3)	47
Mad Broadband (part 4)	48
Now it's the Nazis who are after me	49
Only spammers need apply	51
Dear Santa	53
Smoking in offices is good for business	55

Within easy commuting distance of Dublin	57
More spams, and my reply	59
The sweet smell of success	63
Our council has gone round the bend	65
Greetings to the CIA	66
There is no light at the end of the tunnel	67
All I want for Christmas	69
New traffic system coming to Ireland	71
Foundations laid for new city	72
Wanted – translator for corner shop	74
A Rough Guide to Ireland for Americans	75
Real Reality Television	77
Could you answer a few questions please?	79
Please hold the line for two weeks	81
Come on Ireland – wake up	83
Big Brother is a conspiracy	84
New tunnel for Cork	86
In search of lost punts	88
What would they know anyway?	89
The curse of the century	90
EU legalises hypocrisy	92
New dogs are learning old tricks	94
The day of the Eclipse	95
You look down on me, then I'll look down on you	97
Lament for a dying breed	99
The old tricks are the best	100
2 April 2207	102
A hump or a hole?	104
Neighbours	106
Easter Traditions	107

My Dad	109
Sartorial Elegance	111
The Devil Wears Prada but doesn't speak English	113
Mobile phones	117
Ireland of the Welcomes	119
Seán	121
Puppychild	122
Hang a right and chill out	124
Old-style shopping	126
Holidays	128
Routine	129
And the winner is ...	131
What is the point?	133
Stop the world – I want to get off	134
A floating voter finally sinks	137
A little retrospection	138
Anyone for tee?	139
Electricity is the spark of life	141
Get rid of the remote control	142
Let there be light	144
Plug and play my backside	145
Cheffy's vomit	146
The road less travelled	148
Nostalgia isn't what it used to be	149
How to improve your aim in life	151
Thelma and Louise, Irish style	152
The night I died, but didn't	153
Neighbours	155
Sredliub	156
Waiting	157

New policy for tourists	158
The decline of the village	159
Odds and Ends	160
Count your blessings	161
Neat and tidy	163
Pros and Cons	164
In the heat of the moment	167
An explanation	168
I'm older than I look and I'm younger than I feel	170
Your three minutes are up	172
Side effects	174
Please phone me so I can screw you	174
A rose by any other name	176
My apologies	177
Smoking makes you live longer	178
My loving daughter	179
If it ain't broke – fix it	180
Good things come in small parcels	182
How to disembowel a bus	184
Wherefore art thou, Ron?	186
A choice between two terrorists	187
Ireland is the fastest country in Europe	188
Listen hard to the silence	190
Satisfactory tests	192
A quiet mug of coffee	193
Put that finger there and we will never speak again	194
A change in voting patterns	196
How to get rid of a wasps' nest	197
Living can be fatal	198
Are you a Bum Puffer?	199

Training for assassination	200
Rambles in the hills	201
God to sue America	202
How not to look like a tourist	204
Computers are a curse	206
Christmas is over at last	208
Linux is a load of Billux	210
Yesterday was Friday and tomorrow is Monday	211
Smoking is good for you	212
I will have to grindle Linux	214
Daniel O'Donnell has his uses	215
It was a dark and windy night	216
I've got you under my skin	217
Will it last until 2067?	218
Linux or Windows?	221

*To my wife Celine [Herself]
who fortunately has a great sense of humour*

INTRODUCTION

A couple of years ago, I was messing around on that Internet thingy, and I discovered it was possible to write a sort of on-line diary. There were a lot of people doing it. They were telling us all about their company, or they were giving out recipes. Some were talking about knitting, and some people were talking about things I didn't understand at all.

I decided I would start writing my own little diary. It's not a sort of diary where I go into graphic detail about how I put the cat out, because I don't have a cat. Nor is it the kind of diary where I make notes about when my library books are due back, because I find it is easier to forget. Being 'of an age' I feel a bit alienated by the modern generation and I started writing about all the things that annoyed me. Sometimes I just write about idle thoughts that cross my mind. Sometimes, I will even get a bit senile and will start to reminisce, which must be terribly boring for everyone. But I don't care. That is why I call it *Head Rambles*. It is just about the thoughts that ramble around in my head.

So, who am I?

I'm nobody really. I'm one grain of sand on the desert of life. They call me Grandad, because I am one. I have two lovely grandchildren. I live up in the mountains in the east of Ireland, in a little village called Glendore. You won't find Glendore on any map, because when the Ordnance Surveyors came around, we mistook them for tourists and shot them. They ended up in the landfill with the rest.

It's a peaceful little village. I live there, along with Herself and Sandy, the dog. There are various other people who I may or may not mention, such as our daughter Caitríona (or K8 as she sometimes likes to call herself), and her partner The Accidental Terrorist, or TAT.

I grew up in the Ireland of the 1950s and 1960s when times where harder, but you could buy a box of matches for a penny. Life seemed to be a lot simpler then. The main thing about life in those days was that people left you alone. Now we are into the era of the Nanny State, where we are constantly being protected against ourselves. This drives me up the walls (though there is probably a law against that).

Incidentally, if any of you are worried about my references to shooting tourists, this is just a harmless sport (unless you're a tourist) that we enjoy in the valleys and glens of the mountains. Every man must have a sport. Also it prevents foreigners moving in and spoiling our way of life and pushing house prices beyond local reach.

All I want now is to be left in peace, to smoke my pipe and to enjoy an odd pint of stout. Of course, that is now illegal, just about everywhere in Ireland, but at least our village has the sense to apply laws that are reasonable and to ignore all those petty little regulations that are designed to save us from our own natural inclinations to enjoy ourselves.

MY COUNTY COUNCIL LIKES ME

For years now, I have become used to the phenomenon of occasionally coming across 'temporary traffic lights' which have been placed on each side of some bit of roadworks. You know the ones. They stay red for about five minutes so that you can read a book or admire the workmen having their tea break, and then they change to green (the lights, not the workmen) just about long enough to get in gear before changing to red again.

I used to come across these a few times a year. Now, suddenly, they are everywhere. I did one shortish journey recently and had to go through eight sets. It was handy as I was able to catch up on my reading. I read through quite a few chapters on that one journey. I have found one road out of my area that is still light free, but I suppose it is only a matter of time.

I wrote to the local county council to thank them for the lights, saying that it was nice to be able to relax for a five-minute break every couple of miles. They obviously appreciated this, as they promptly gave me my own set. No kidding! Two days later they erected temporary traffic lights on each side of the entrance to my house and started digging holes. Now that is service.

HOW TO SURVIVE YOUR FIRST GUINNESS

Most visitors to Ireland can't wait to try a real pint of Guinness. They are right. It's the only country where you can get a *real* pint. The foreign stuff is the slop they scrape off the top. They have to get rid of it somewhere.

However, your first pint is potentially the most lethal trap you will have to encounter. 99% of tourists give themselves away on this one. So here is how to do it.

Enter the pub. Look nonchalant. Don't look as if you are about to have a life-changing experience. Walk casually to the bar and wait. Don't call the barman. Don't rap a coin on the counter. That will annoy him, and you don't want to do that at this stage. He'll come to you. If he speaks with a foreign accent, get the fuck out of there. He won't know how to pull a pint.

He'll ask you what you want. Just say 'pint, please'. If he asks 'a pint of what?', then scowl at him and snarl 'Guinness, of course.' Most barmen won't ask anyway, as Guinness is the 'pint' by default. He will then take a pint glass and fill it about two-thirds to three-quarters full and place it on the counter.

First trap

LEAVE THE DRINK THERE. DON'T TOUCH IT! The barman will probably walk away. Don't mind that. Just stare into the distance. Go have a pee or a quick fag. But you must wait.

After a minute or two, he will come back and top it up to a full pint. Again DO NOTHING. Just wait. He will tinker around with it for a moment, and will eventually bring it over to you. If he has engraved a shamrock in the head of the pint, then I suggest you sit down and write out your Last Will and Testament. You are as good as dead. The barman has spotted that you are a tourist and has flagged you. The locals look for this and will be quietly loading ammunition into their guns.

Second trap

(Assuming you are still alive): DON'T TOUCH THE PINT. It will still be settling. You have to wait until there is a crisp demarcation line between the black and the white. The longer you wait, the better. At this stage, it is perfectly acceptable to stare at the pint.

Third trap

The locals will be watching you to see how you approach the pint. If you try and slurp the white head off (or even worse, blow it off) you have signed your death certificate. The chances are that you will be hung off the wall and the locals will use you as a dartboard for the rest of the night.

Another fatal error is to sip the pint. Sipping is for nancies and their glasses of wine. This is Guinness, for fuck sake. You grasp the glass firmly in your fist and gulp back at least a quarter, if not a third of the contents. Act like this is the first drink you've had since coming out of the desert (which it is).

At this stage, the locals will begin to relax. You are quite entitled to burp at this stage (actually, it's unavoidable), but don't do it too loudly.

If you are a wimp, and don't like the taste, DON'T SHOW IT. Keep calm. Nip up and order a whiskey. That is acceptable. It's called a Chaser. But you must finish the pint before knocking back the whiskey. (Which would you rather? Drinking a Guinness, or being shot?).

The chances are, you will like it. You can relax now. You can now savour it a mouthful at a time.

To really convince the locals that you are not a tourist, wait until you have about 2 inches left in the glass. Then catch the barman's eye and raise one finger. This is the signal to start processing the next pint. This should arrive just as you finish the first.

Of course this now means that you have to continue ordering pints. Don't worry about it. You have survived, and that is something to celebrate (if you need an excuse, that is).

All this has made me thirsty. I think I'll go and have a pint or five.

ANSWER THIS ONE

Herself was listening to the radio yesterday morning. I didn't hear the programme myself, so I'm going by what she said.

Apparently there was an American complaining about the smoking regime here. He was appalled that the smoking areas outside some pubs were so comfortable. He complained that smokers were being too well catered for. He complained that smokers seemed to be enjoying themselves.

He couldn't understand how they were not ashamed to be seen smoking.

Holy shit! What kind of arrogant sanctimonious self-righteous bigots are the anti-smoking lobby becoming? What is wrong with smoking?

Before you start, don't give me any of that health crap. Show me one person who has definitively died of passive smoking. I have never heard of one. I have heard of many who have died of cancer without ever being near a cigarette though. So any figures you throw up are entirely without foundation.

Don't talk to me about litter. Someone who throws cigarette butts around is just as likely to throw anything else around. Don't talk to me about respiratory ailments. The only time I ever had those was when I worked in the city centre and had to breathe exhaust fumes all day. You can talk to me about damage to *my own* health. But that's my business.

Do please talk to me about alcohol. Let's talk about the litter *that* causes – the broken families, the crime, the drink driving, the rapes, the street fighting, the assaults, the wife battering and all the rest. Go to an A&E on a Saturday night and show me how many battered and damaged bodies are brought in and show me which ones are caused by smoking and which by alcohol.

I know life would be better without tobacco. But it would be a lot safer without alcohol, or chemicals, or cars, or planes, or DIY tools, or sport. More people die on a golf course than from passive smoking.

Please, I beg of you. Please tell me why smoking is more dangerous than alcohol.

So, let's get our priorities right. Let's ban the things that cause real harm, if you are so concerned about health. Or are you? Or have you just been brainwashed by the Politically Correct tide?

IN THE DARK

I got a postcard today. That was nice. It means someone cares.

However, this postcard was from the ESB. They would like to inform me that they are cutting off my power in a couple of week's time. No. I have paid my bills. They are cutting me off for a day. From 9 a.m. to 6 p.m. Something to do with connecting people.

This fills me with dread. They have done this before and it is not nice. It's amazing how much I rely on electricity for the simple pleasures in life like heat or a nice cup of tea. A day is very long when you can't have a cuppa. My theory is that time is relative, but is determined by how much power you have. Actually, I would like to have a word with Einstein about this but he isn't around. A normal 9 a.m. to 6 p.m. day here lasts approximately nine hours (give or take). However, without power I swear it lasts over twenty-four hours. Maybe industry should take note of this – cut off power to the factory floor and get an extra fifteen hours work from the labour force.

In the meantime, what am I going to do on THE day? In the old days, I would have gone to the nearest pub and gotten rat-arsed. But I'm too old for that now. And I would have to spend the entire time outside because the Health Police have decided that I'm a hazard to the workforce (doubtless I'll have a comment or two in the future about smoking laws).

If the weather is nice, I might go for a walk. But that won't take too long. I might do a bit of gardening (but it is never nice on the day of a power cut). I might visit my daughter, but she has her own life to lead.

Anyone got a spare generator?

NOT A GRUMP

It is time my Sandy had a mention on the Internet. She is one of the most intelligent and faithful dogs I have ever come across, and I've known a few.

She's learning to drive at the moment. She sits in the passenger seat and watches everything I do. She is also very critical of other drivers and gives me a knowing look if she sees an example of bad driving. If I leave her in the car for a while, she sits in the driver's seat and practises the controls.

The only thing in life she hates is loud noises. She hates thunder or fireworks. They reduce her to a quivering jelly and she has to go and hide under the sideboard. I hate this time of year (Hallowe'en is around the corner) as there is the occasional firework most evenings. It only takes one and she's gone. It could be worse though. We could be living in the suburbs where the fireworks in the lead-up to Hallowe'en would make Iraq seem like the Garden of Eden.

In the meantime, there is nothing she likes better than to curl up in bed with a good book.

PEOPLE OUT THERE REALLY LIKE ME

I get lots of emails. Hundreds of them. Often I think they are a little confused because they keep wanting my banking details for banks I've never heard of, but we all make mistakes.

I also get mails for very nice people who want to meet me. They usually start off with something like 'Hi, I am a very good-looking girl and would like to meet you'. That's nice. But a lot of them come from people called George or John. I think someone should tell them what a good-looking girl looks like. I wouldn't say girls with beards and hairy chests would be *very* good-looking.

I got one today. The title (at the risk of offending some people) is 'My penis has grown from 3 inches to just over 6 inches, and is still growing!' Fair play says I. But it is sent by 'Fumiko Lady'. Now there is a girl with a problem. And apparently it's growing! I don't know why she is telling *me* about it though.

The really good news is that I keep winning lotteries. I estimate that at the time of writing, I am worth somewhere in the region of €300 million. One of these days when I'm running a little short of cash, I'll write back to these nice people and ask for my money.

If I'd known there were such lovely people around, I never would have bothered with a pension plan.

PUT YOUR WALLET AWAY. I'LL GET THIS

I don't believe it. I really don't believe it. This country is in a mess. At least it is as far as the health service, education and welfare go. We have hospitals that remain closed because they can't afford to run 'em. We have people lying on trolleys in emergency departments. We have people dying because their nearest hospital doesn't have the right facilities. We have an almost non-existent support for people with special needs. We have the elderly being abused in homes. We have schools falling down around the kids' ears. And all because we don't have the money to spend.

Then I pick up the paper today, and what do I see? 'Dublin to spend €1bn in North'. And a lot of that is going to healthcare and provision of facilities in a Derry hospital.

Now, I'm all for good relations with the North. I have the greatest respect for the people there. I like holidaying there. I would ultimately like to see a (peaceful) complete integration. I'm a supporter of the latest initiatives. But the fact remains, it is still technically a foreign country. It still has a monarchy, uses sterling and has its own laws. And we are paying for their health and the upgrading of their roads?

Or is the government just trying to look good, and they are hoping the cheque will be refused because it's in euro?

What is going on here? I must be misunderstanding something. Is the whole world going mad or is it just me?

I'VE BEEN ZEROED

I bought a car last year. It's a second-hand Focus that was two years old, but in pristine condition. I got a Focus because Herself wanted one. It wouldn't have been my first choice, but I'm glad I got it.

Earlier this year, I was pootling along the motorway when I checked my speed. I like to *try* to keep within the speed limits. To my amazement I was doing 0. And my rev-counter said 0 too. And I was apparently out of petrol (having filled up the previous day). Something wrong here, thinks I. Then I realised all the instruments had failed (I can be slow on the uptake sometimes).

It is tricky driving when you don't know what speed you are doing. Too slow and you run the risk of road rage from the trucker behind you. Too fast and it's a few more points on the old licence. I found the best answer was to tuck in behind the slowest driver I could find. Then I could explain to the trucker that it was them that was holding us up.

I got it fixed a few days later. It cost a fortune as the whole unit had to be replaced. Funny how they can never 'fix' things these days – they always 'have to replace the unit'. It cost me an arm and a leg despite my protests that it was only just out of warranty. However I was glad to get the car back and paid up. They pointed out that I now had a metric speedometer, as if this was some kind of consolation.

Actually it was. I can now legally overtake a lot of cars. Because people are driving with speedometers showing miles per hour and they have to mentally convert from the old money to new, they tend to err on the side of caution.

The other side effect of the repair is that the garage forgot to reset my mileage counter. When I collected it, it was at zero. As the Americans would say – Yeeehawww! (I don't know why they say that, but in this case it seems appropriate.)

Anyone like to buy a three-year-old car with a genuine 3,000 on the clock?

EXPERIENCE DESIRED, BUT NOT ESSENTIAL

The scene: An interview room in a large state company. There is a bored looking interviewer waiting for the candidate. The candidate enters. He has a shaved head and is wearing an Ireland football shirt, tattered jeans and scruffy runners. He farts loudly, sits down and starts to pick his nose. A distinct smell of alcohol and old socks begins to fill the room.

The interviewer sighs, but protocol says he has to complete the interview.

Interviewer: 'This interview is for a top position in a prestigious state company that has a considerable influence on the fiscal situation pertaining at the moment. Could you elaborate on your suitability for this position?'
Candidate: 'What?'
Interviewer: 'Why did you apply for the job?'
Candidate: 'Me mate told me to.'

The interviewer sighs again: 'What educational qualifications do you have?'

Candidate: 'I have me Junior Cert. I done the Group Cert when I was in the Joy but didn't get that.'
Interviewer: 'And why were you in Mountjoy Prison?'
Candidate: 'I done three years for the joyridin' and another eight for sellin' H down Pearse Street Flats. Dey let me out early cause dey were overcrowded. But me mate might have had sumpthin to do with that too.'
Interviewer: 'And what employment experience do you have?'
Candidate: 'Employment? Ah jayzus dere's no need to work. I have de dole and the micky money from the ten kids, and I send de mot Jacinta out to do de cleaning. It pays for de chips and de Budweiser.'
Interviewer: 'And pastimes?'
Candidate: 'Ah, I back a few horses and hang around. I have a load af pints with me mate over in Drumcondra.'

Interviewer: 'Who is this "mate" you keep on about?'
Candidate: 'Me mate Bertie. Has The Big Job in de government. I loaned him a few quid a while ago, and he said he owed me one. He told me to go for this job.'
Interviewer: 'Welcome to the board sir. We are currently redecorating your executive suite so there is no need to start immediately. Is 300 grand a year enough or would you like more?'

LIFE FROM THE VIEWPOINT OF A GOLDFISH

I have a problem. I was going to write about something today, but I've forgotten what it was.

Bugger. I have discovered that this is one of the pains and pleasures of getting old. The memory starts playing tricks. It becomes erratic. I haven't quite reached the stage where I forget to put my trousers on before going out, but I have come close. I suppose that day will come. It won't be funny for me, but the neighbours will have a laugh.

I always had a strange memory. I could never remember names or faces. I remember a name for the length of time it takes to say it. I have an 'I know that face from somewhere' moment in the street only to realise later it was my brother. But numbers? Give me a number and I'm OK. I know my phone number, my credit card number, my bank account numbers, my library card numbers, every phone number I ever had (If anyone is interested, my first number phone was back in the 1950s – 907339. Don't bother ringing it – they changed them all in the 1960s). No problem at all with numbers.

It's true what they say about long-term and short-term memory as you get older. I could give you graphic day by day accounts of my pre-school days, but don't ask me what I watched on telly last night. Not that the latter is a good example – 99% of telly these days is instantly forgettable anyway.

One of the good things about this is that we have an endless supply of good films on TV. People complain that they are all re-runs, but we don't care. We have forgotten that we watched them so we can watch them all over again. I get the odd *déjà vu* moment when watching a film and realise at the very end that I *had* seen it before (three times), but what the heck.

Unfortunately this doesn't apply to books. I read a lot. And I mean a *lot*. But I get books out of the library, because I don't recognise the author or the plot, and then get home to realise after the first couple of pages that I have read it before. Hate that.

I lose things too. I can walk from A to B in the house and somewhere in between I'll put down my pipe or whatever. When I reach B I find the pipe is gone, and have to retrace my steps and try to remember where I've been.

Luckily we have two phones, but one is a mobile and the other is a wireless handset. The keyword here is 'wireless'. It isn't tied down, so it gets lost. Again, many happy moments wandering around the house with one phone ringing the other until we hear the lost one warbling from under the couch, or under the dog's blanket. I just wish the remote controls had phone numbers, so we could find them as easily.

Herself is worse. She goes off and buys her fags and puts them away somewhere. We then spend many happy hours looking for them as she has forgotten. They usually turn up in the deep freeze or the coalhole or somewhere like that.

Happy days.

GO KICK YOUR BALLS BEFORE I DO

I'm going to ruffle a few feathers here. I know I'm in the minority, so statistically I'm going to annoy at least 100% of my three readers. Maybe more. But it is a subject that has plagued me all my life. Not just in the autumn of my years.

'What is he on about?' you ask.

'Sport,' says I.

Now don't get me wrong. I'm not against sport as such. It is very healthy for the kids to go out and kick a ball around the local playing field. Running is good too. It comes in handy when you are about to miss the bus, or when the girlfriend's husband comes home unexpectedly.

What really irritates me is the obsession with sport. I hate sport personally and that is my right. You like sport and that is your right. Just stop ramming it down my throat.

Take it off the telly. Stop talking about it except among yourselves.

There is an assumption that we all love sport. There is a sport slot on every RTÉ news broadcast. Why isn't there a gardening slot too? Or a pet lover's spot? ('Today, Tiddles gave birth to five kittens. We go live now to our reporter outside the vet's surgery.') Every day we have to sit and listen to some prat waffling on through a list of sports. And there are so many. Soccer, GAA, rugby, athletics, motor-racing, golf. The list is bloody endless. And we have to get the inane details. The exact results of every horse race, the endless lists of soccer scores, how Beckham has chipped another fingernail …

Soccer is the worst. Endless programmes devoted to it. I can't go into the pub without someone asking what I thought of the game last night. I don't care about the game last night. I didn't see it. I was too busy trying to find a channel that wasn't showing it.

And if the game isn't bad enough, we have to wade through the analysis. 'And what do you think the result would have been if he had missed that goal?' I ask you! All sports commentators seem to have the intelligence of amoebas. (Sorry, amoebas. I don't mean to insult you.) I swear to God I heard one say recently: 'Ireland scored their first goal after only two minutes, but from then on things went from bad to worse'. They have so many clichés that they throw them in without thinking.

And they are devoting their energies to talking about soccer players as if they were gods. Cop on! Soccer players are simple-minded blokes who can only do one thing in life, and that is to kick a bit of plastic around a field. And they are paid sums of money that are frightening. A premiership footballer earns more in one hour that an African family can expect to earn in fifty generations. They are not worth it. Most of them have an intelligence rating that is so poor that if they dropped one point on the IQ scale, you'd have to water them. They are a bunch of prima donnas who burst into tears if someone touches them.

Another thing is the Irish obsession with British football. I know blokes who still rant on about the famine and the Brit occupation of our fair land for the last 600 years. But next thing you see them, wearing their Liverpool or Manchester United shirts and roaring at the telly as if their lives depended on it. It's getting so bad that people are naming their kids after players. Why not name them after your favourite flower? ('Have you met my son Convallaria Majalis Murphy?')

The worst of the lot is the World Cup. Every four years I lose the will to live. It goes on and on and on and on. Everyone is talking about it. The newspapers and the TV are full of it. You'd think it was Christ's second coming. I say every four years, but there is now a two year run up to it. And when you think it is over for another four years, they start on about the Olympics. Oh God!

If you like sport so much, why don't you just get out a ball and kick it around the road. Preferably the M50.

HOLY SMOKE! OIREACHTAS REPORT IS FUNNY!

Another introduction. This time it's my daughter's turn. I can't post a photograph of her on the Net because the last time I did, she was rather angry.

She is a lovely girl. She is tall, beautiful, a great cook, and has a great sense of humour. Most important though – she likes her old dad. We get on very well. She is great fun to have around. I love her very much.

She also brings me presents from time to time. Earlier in the year she gave me a load of plants for the conservatory, which was nice. They weren't very nice looking, but I didn't want to hurt her feelings. I looked up the plants in my handbook but couldn't find them, which was strange. They grew beautifully. They became enormous and blocked most of the light out of the conservatory. Also they smelled a bit strange. But they were a present, and I was too sentimental to throw them out.

However, after a few months they began to look sad. The leaves turned brown and the smell was overpowering, so I decided that it was time for them to go. We aren't allowed bonfires in the garden any more so I burned them in the grate. They burned very well, but they made the chimney smoke a bit, so that made our eyes water.

The reason I remember that night so well is that it was the night we discovered 'Oireachtas Report' on RTÉ. That was one of the funniest programs I ever saw. It was up there with *Reggie Perrin* and *Fawlty Towers*. We screamed with laughter. We wet ourselves. It was hilarious. Actually most of the programmes on RTÉ were funny that night, which is unusual.

I phoned my daughter the next day to confess that I had thrown out her present. She didn't seem too pleased. I think she called me a skunk, but the line was bad so I'm not sure.

We couldn't wait for the next 'Oireachtas Report'. But it wasn't funny. In fact, it was incredibly boring. They must have changed the scriptwriters.

WHY I HATE THE DAWN CHORUS

I'm sitting here looking out at a beautiful crisp November morning. The sky is clear and blue. There is a lovely frost on the ground. There isn't a breath of wind and the sun is shining. Am I enjoying it? No!

Why not? Because there is a burglar alarm screeching away on the house next door and spoiling the peace. It has been screaming for the last half hour and my head is wrecked.

Why do people have the damned things? They are worse than useless. I have yet to see anyone run to catch a would-be burglar. When an alarm goes off, people just mutter profanities about the owner and then try to ignore it.

As a security device it has the opposite effect. If I were a housebreaker, I would seek out houses where the alarm is going off. I'd know that I was safe. I'd know that the neighbours are all indoors with the windows closed. I'd know that the majority of neighbours are wishing that the house *would* be burgled just to teach the householder a lesson.

I used to live in The City. It was a nightmare there. Every morning we would be woken by the dawn chorus – a cacophony of house alarms and car alarms. There would be bells and sirens and everything in between. Presumably the dimwits would open their front doors to go to work and forget that they had set the alarm. Fair enough to do it once, but *every* morning?

I suppose one good thing is that I now have a new profession in my retirement. Now, where did I leave that crowbar?

PLEASE LEAVE A MESSAGE AFTER THE TONE ...

Half a century ago, communications were nice and simple. You could talk to people, or write a letter, or you could phone them. If things were really urgent, you could send a telegram.

Phones were nice and simple. Not every house had one (it was quite a status symbol). They were bulky Bakelite yokes with dials on. You could wear the tip off your finger if you did much dialling.

Public phones were great. You still had the old Bakelite phone, but there was a big box underneath. You put in your 2d (if you don't know what 2d is, ask your grandparents) and you dialled the number. If the person answered, you pressed button 'A' and got talking. And once you were through, you could talk all day for no extra cost.

If you got the wrong number, or if you suddenly decided you didn't want to talk, you pressed button 'B' and your money shot back out into the little scoop. This was a great source of income to the local kids, as they would stuff a bit of paper up the scoop to block the money. They would then return in the evening, remove the paper and out would shoot all the returned coins. Of course, I never did that.

Things have changed a bit since then. Letters have more or less died a death. That's a pity, because letters had the personal touch. You knew someone cared enough to take the trouble to write. Now it's all emails. Impersonal. A tap of the fingers and it's gone. I know it's fast and convenient, but I miss the handwriting.

And some twit invented mobile phones. The curse of the modern age. Now every five-year-old seems to have one. And they are not just phones. They're cameras, and calculators and even mobile computers. They are everywhere. I have seen mothers phone their kids in the supermarket, to find which aisle the child is in. 'I'm at the freezer section. Are you over at the baked beans?'

There is no peace any more. You can be sitting chatting to someone and their pocket starts warbling a strangled version of Madonna or the 1812 overture. And they whip it out and start a conversation in front of you. Weird. You go down to the pub for a quiet pint and these yokes are buzzing and wailing all around you. You sit on the bus or the train and there is always some prat yelling into his mobile that they are on the bus or the train. Who cares?

And kids can't spell any more because they use texting language. They spend their time texting each other what a gr8 nite they had with their m8s. They even have become so brain dead that they send emails using text-speak, as if it is clever. No. It's a sign of illiteracy and lack of respect for the recipient.

I confess, I have a mobile. I didn't want one, but it was given to me. I only give the number to close friends. I admit it does come in handy if I'm delayed somewhere and I want to let someone know I'll be late. And if I want peace and quiet, or more importantly if I'm visiting someone, I turn it off.

I just wish it had a button 'B'.

DOES MY BUM LOOK BIG IN THIS?

Some time ago, Herself decided to order some – what shall we call them? – intimate undergarments. She chose a company in the UK and asked me to order them on-line for her. I had no problem with this. I do most of the on-line buying anyway. Even the groceries. So I duly filled out the order form, and was very careful to enter *her* name and our address.

The company was very efficient. The order arrived swiftly, and it was precisely what Herself wanted. It came in a nice package with a friendly letter inside. The package was even nicely decorated so that, while being discreet, it left no doubt as to the contents. And here is where the problem started.

You see, I had used my own credit card which (of course) had my name on it. I had also used my own email address. Now they obviously took the credit card name as being the customer. A reasonable assumption. So the parcel arrived addressed to me. I also received an email saying they hoped the garments fitted all right.

My mother always taught me to reply to letters, so I wrote back to the nice lady, thanking her for the order and her nice email. I told her that I hadn't actually tried the garments on yet as I was the wrong shape. I did tell her though that Herself was wearing them and was delighted. She apologised. She said they would change the name in their computer. She never did though.

Since then Herself has ordered a lot more 'items' from the same place. They always come addressed to me. I get nice brochures from them too, in clear plastic envelopes. I also get emails from them with nice pictures of pretty ladies wearing nearly nothing.

I hope the police don't raid my computer, or I'll be down as a sex offender. And the postman gives me very strange looks. In fact he has taken to throwing our post through the letterbox and running away. And I can't go into the Post Office at all.

It has its upside though. I've just received a lovely email from them advertising 'The Trinny and Susannah Magic Knickers' with before and after photographs. I've a choice of 'The Tummy Flatner Thong', 'The Bum Lifter' or 'The Bum, Tum and Thigh Reducer'. I can't decide which would suit me best …

ON THE ROAD TO NOWHERE

It has happened again.

I went down for the paper and someone asked me for directions. Do I look like a walking Ordnance Survey? I must do, because it is virtually impossible to stray outside without being asked for directions to here or there.

Now you have to understand the area where I live. It is very scenic, but it is a maze of winding roads, with junctions all over the place. Some of those junctions are farm tracks and not roads, and other junctions are nicely hidden on bends. And of course our county council don't really believe in road signs. They think signs would detract from the charm of the area. Maybe they're right, but it means a lot of people get lost.

It is a nightmare giving directions. It's not a simple 'go down to the end of that road and you're on the motorway'. It's more of a 'go up that road 'til you come to a junction with a big house on the left. Turn right, but not sharp right because that's Paddy's farm. Immediately past the graveyard on your left there is a hidden junction on the right. Take that etc. etc.' Do you see what I mean?

I used to give long detailed instructions that were accurate, but I knew they were confused. On a couple of occasions, I told them to jump into the car and I'd bring them. They were delighted, until we arrived at their destination and they remembered they had a car and now had to walk all the way back.

Then I started to get lazy, and I'd just send them down to the village and tell them to ask someone there.

Now I'm getting old and nasty. I just send them up to the top of the road. It's so easy. 'Yes. You are on the right road. Keep going straight on this road for about five miles'. That brings them up to the top of the mountains. It is a complete wilderness up there. There is nothing except mile after mile of bog. You can drive for an hour without even seeing a sheep. It is very beautiful and the views are fantastic. But you are unlikely to find your way out.

There are probably several dozen tourists up there by now, of different nationalities. They are still looking for their destinations, but of course there is no one to ask. Maybe they meet one another from time to time and swap stories.

So here is a message for anyone intending to visit my area. Bring a very detailed map. Do not stop and ask that tall bloke with a grey beard and pipe for directions. Unless of course you like bogs.

TAKE TWO BEFORE GOING TO SCHOOL

I feel so sorry for the children of today. They have to contend with so many things that didn't exist when I was a lad.

For a start there is depression. That didn't exist in my day. If I felt a bit down, I was sent out into the garden to chop wood. It made me feel better. I could 'vent my spleen', as they say. I could get rid of all my frustrations on an unfortunate block of timber. Now the poor mites have to take Valium and Prozac to help them cope. Ahhhhh!

Then there is stress. Oh yes. We did have stress. It was usually caused by either a) being late for school because we were slow getting up or b) not having done/finished our homework. I was stressed every morning of my school life (for reasons 'a' *and* 'b'). I arrived late for school and got leathered for that, and then went up to the classroom where I got leathered for not having my homework. That was life. That was daily routine. That was stress. I lived, and got a good education. Now the kids aren't allowed stress. Poor things. They are given more Valium and Prozac.

Another modern invention is Attention Deficit Disorder. Come on! In my day that was called 'being disruptive'. It meant you were a pain in the ~~arse~~ classroom. It was rightly your fault and you got clattered for it. (In my day, you got clattered/leathered for nearly everything). Nowadays, the little dears have 'problems' that have to have labels, so they are rushed off to their psychiatrist where they are told they have ADD or some such, and given more Valium and Prozac.

In my day, if you gave cheek to the teacher, you were:
- Given a belt around the head
- Given the leather
- Given 500 lines
- Sent outside the door
- Sent to the headmaster
- All of the above

Now if you give cheek to the teacher, it means you must have some underlying psychological problem. You are given more Prozac and Valium.

If something traumatic happened in our lives, we shrugged and got on with life. Now they have to have counselling and are doubtless given Valium and Prozac, to help them get over it.

Having survived the school system while being doped up to the eyeballs in tranquillisers and whatnot, modern children are then berated for experimenting with drugs. Am I the only person who sees a connection here?

AFTERNOON COFFEE

Herself wanted to go to the village yesterday for a pack of fags. We drove down and I parked in front of the coffee shop. I knew that buying a pack of fags was going to take at least an hour, if not longer. Herself is like that.

So I got my mug and settled down outside. It was bloody cold, but one must make sacrifices if one wants a puff on the pipe these days. At least the tables weren't crowded.

It was very pleasant (apart from the cold). I even met some friends I hadn't seen in years.

Of course I was asked for directions.

The first was a motorcyclist. I don't like motorcyclists since they started wearing those black balls on their heads, so I sent him up to the bogs at the top of the mountains.

The second was an old man who was even older than me. He was on foot, so I couldn't send him up to the bogs. I told him how to get to the place he was looking for, but of course sent him by the long route.

Our Sandy (the dog) was in the car, which was beside me. If I leave her in the car, she moves to the driver's seat. You can see she feels important. She sits there as if waiting for a passenger to return, looking very solemn.

Some tourists came by. You know the type – all cameras and huge backsides. What they were doing here in November is anyone's guess.

'Aw gee Honey. Look at the cute little doggie who thinks he's driving the auto?'

Honey stepped into the road in front of the car to photograph Sandy. I couldn't resist it. I stepped over and tapped him on the shoulder.

'Word of advice, pal,' says I. 'If she starts the engine, get back on the footpath quick. She's well known around here as a reckless driver.'

The tourists didn't know what to say or think. They ran.

Sandy grinned. She loves a good laugh.

OH FOR THE OPEN ROAD

Herself wanted to go to the city on Wednesday. I said no. She demanded. I shut her in the coalhole.

She thanked me after, because that day, Ireland had its worst ever traffic jam in history. Mind you, records only go back to the middle of the nineteenth century, so there may have been longer ones before that. But I doubt it.

Apparently a man dug a hole on the hard shoulder of the N11 in Bray, while eighteen men watched him. Note that this was the hard shoulder, not part of the road. But they put up thousands of cones anyway. What the heck. They're cheap.

Now, no one thought to tell anyone about this. The gardaí didn't know. The AA was very slow on the uptake. But not as slow as the drivers who got stuck in the jam. The jam eventually stretched back for fifteen miles along the M11 and the M50. Some of these people were stuck for over seven hours.

There were women with babies. There were women about to give birth. There were people trying to get to meetings. There were old people. There were people just trying to get home. And none of them had food or water. Or toilets.

Now when you get to my age, the first thing you think of when you get stuck in a jam, is 'Thank God I don't need a pee'. Of course that thought brings on the urge. And how do you hold onto an urge for six hours?

And all of this was caused by a bloke digging a hole.

Now some people got wind of this and took to the back roads. But of course they were laying pipes there so the roads were all ripped up.

So some took to the mountains, but they were making a film up there so the road was closed.

So that basically left one road south. But a bloke was digging a hole. The entire south of Dublin and north Wicklow came to a standstill. Herself has promised that the next time she wants to go to the city, she'll lock herself in the coalhole.

MAD BROADBAND (PART 1)

I've been having a little bit of trouble with my Internet connection. It has been grand for a long time, but it started to get a bit hairy this week. I asked my friend Ron about it and he suggested I phone the company.

So I rang them. I went through all the usual automatic switchboard rubbish and the piped music but finally got to speak to someone. I told him my problem. He did some tweaky things at his end and came up with the diagnosis (it's wonderful what they can do with computers these days).

'Your aerial is faulty, and we'll have to come out and fix it,' says he. Fair enough.

Yesterday they called out. It was lashing rain and I felt a bit sorry for them, but they set to work anyway. They found the problem straight away.

'Trees have grown into the line of the signal.'

So I got out my binoculars and showed them the mast in the distance. It was a bit misty but we could see it. There were no trees in the way!

They cursed (in Polish, I think). They beavered away, running up and down ladders and in and out of the house and muttering about technical thingies. They got more and more annoyed looking. They didn't seem to be doing much apart from making a mess of my floor. They rang their office a few times. They tried different aerials. They tried moving the aerial around a bit. They rang their office a few more times. They eventually came up to me with big smiles on their faces and gave me the good news.

'We are sorry but the signal is not available in your area. We are going to remove all the equipment.'

I turned purple. Herself grabbed the phone in case the doctor might be necessary.

'But I have had good service for a long time and it has only just failed, and you are not removing my equipment.'

'Yes,' says he, 'but the signal is not available.'

Here was one of these 'I've found my story and I'm sticking to it' chaps. I demanded to speak to an engineer on the phone. When I spoke to him, the engineer said the same thing.

'We are sorry, but the signal is not available in your area.'

I was dangerously near a heart attack at this stage. I restrained myself and patiently explained that I had great service up to this week and it had only just failed. He tried to persuade me that it had been failing since September.

'Tuesday,' says I.

So he sighed and asked to speak to one of the lads again. They muttered in a huddle and said they would try again. They faffed around a bit and did all the things they had done before. Then I realised that they were on the phone to the engineer again. I grabbed the phone.

'What the flip [or words to that effect] is going on?' says I.

He gave me a lot of bullshit and said that the lads were going to restore the system and leave.

'It's fixed,' says the lads.

I tested the signal on my PC. It was exactly the same as before they arrived.

'It's not fixed. It's the ******* same ******** service as I had before you ******** came!' says I.

43

They left anyway. I phoned the office and raised merry hell. When I get going, I am a sight to behold. I am used as an example in most anger management schools (what not to say). I finally got it out of a manager. They had 'upgraded the system to enhance the service for existing and future customers, and this had degraded my signal so that it was no longer viable.'

'That doesn't make sense. I am an existing customer and my service hasn't been enhanced!'

'Sorry about that,' says he, 'but some of our remoter customers will lose service.'

'But the upgrade took place last Thursday and my service was grand 'til Tuesday.'

'No,' says he, 'you had very bad service since Thursday'.

There was really no getting through to this bloke.

At this stage, the steam coming out my ears could have driven Poolbeg Power Station. Herself was trying to insert a Prozac drip-feed into my arm.

'Let me get this straight,' says I. 'I have a contract with you people. I have been getting a great service up 'til Tuesday with no complaints whatsoever. Now you "upgraded" the service on the 16th to improve it. Since then I have had continuing good service for an additional five days after your tweaking, but now you say that a signal is no longer available in my area?'

'That's right,' says he. 'You never had a good signal. And as a result of the upgrade it is degraded below the level of viability.'

'Would you like to talk about this on the radio?' says I, playing one of my trump cards.

There was a long silence. 'Leave it with me,' says he, 'I'll see what I can do'.

To be continued …

MAD BROADBAND (PART 2)

Well, it has been a busy Saturday and a lot has been happening. My two friends Ron and Dick have more or less moved in to help me. Herself is making the cheese on toast to keep us fed.

Ron's good friend Michele sent us some figures that proved that I have not been lying all along. Apparently Michele has been keeping records of how fast I connect to the Internet. Why she should do this just for me, I don't know. Ron will explain no doubt. Thank you Michele anyway. You sound like a nice girl.

So we wrote a rather gruff letter to the company and enclosed the figures. We explained that they couldn't possibly be telling the truth and that they should get things fixed straight away. Or else. We didn't get a reply.

Dick apparently knows of another case like mine. They complained of a bad connection and our foreign friend came out to them and apparently used exactly the same technique as they tried on me. The gentleman who lived there was at work at the time and his wife believed them. She told them to take the equipment away if it was no good. I believe he wasn't too happy when he came home that evening and found he had no broadband.

Now, this morning an interesting thing happened. Ron and Dick are still here. We made a night of it. Herself is getting a bit cheesed off with the cheese on toast making, and is beginning to complain about all the empty beer cans.

Anyway, Ron and Dick were running some tests. They ran one at around half eleven. There were sharp intakes of breath. Dick told me I was getting 1 meg down but nothing at all up. I was tempted to say that I am used to getting nothing up, but we'll keep the talk technical here. Anyway, he said this was bad. He said it looked like it was all over.

But then he ran another test and nearly passed out. We revived him, and he told us that the signal was excellent. Well, not perfect, but more than adequate. He said it was 1.5 meg down and 1.2 meg up whatever that means.

So Ron and Dick are jumping for joy. I said it mightn't last. They said it didn't matter, because it proved that I could get a decent signal even after all the messing around that the company did, and that all their excuses had fallen flat.

So maybe they have fixed the fault at last? Or maybe they undid whatever it was they did in the first place? Or maybe they are beaming a special signal just to me? Or maybe the CIA intervened because they didn't want to lose track of me? Or maybe they *did* read yesterday's mail?

We'll have to wait 'til tomorrow when I can phone the company and find out what is going on.

Footnote to the above:

I have just received an invoice for next month's service. Oh! Sweet irony!!

MAD BROADBAND (PART 3)

There has been an interesting development. The company rang me.

The engineer was extremely nice to me. He was nearly in tears at the upset they have caused me. I cannot, for the life of me, fathom what brought about this change of heart.

Maybe they read my blog and feel sorry for me? I doubt it. Maybe it was the letter I sent threatening legal action and massive media coverage? Could be. Maybe it was my daughter's boyfriend and his 'friends' rolling up to their head office on the motorbikes, smashing all the windows and daubing 'Save Grandad' all over the walls? Another possibility. Divine intervention? God knows.

Anyway, they are apparently calling out on Wednesday. They are going to send 'their' engineers (as distinct from fellas who haven't a clue) who, I am promised, will speak fluent English. They are going to sort me out if it kills them. Or maybe they are going to sort me out and kill me. One or the other. They are going to be in constant touch with the Head Office engineer. They are going to try everything to get me a decent signal to my existing mast. If they can't do that, they'll try a different mast.

The fella who rang me actually got quite excited. He thinks I'm going to be OK. Not only that but they are going to try to give me faster speeds than I had before. They are coming first thing in the morning. It looks like they are going to make a day of it, so I am laying in plenty of beer and sandwiches. (For me, you fool. Not them.)

MAD BROADBAND (PART 4)

Hopefully, this is the end of the saga.

I shinned up onto the roof yesterday. Herself gave out stink, saying I could fall off the roof at my age. Anyway, I had a good old poke around with the binoculars. And when I had finished peering into various neighbours gardens and windows, I had a look for my alternative mast. The pair I had out on Friday said it couldn't be seen. They had looked everywhere, but there were trees in the way. But there it was. Clear as crystal. I think those two couldn't see the world for the trees.

The broadband company arrived in force. They had a van and a cherry picker, but they had to leave the latter in the village because they'd never get it in my gate.

I brought them up on the roof. I showed them the mast. 'That looks like it,' says they.

They were like that last pair – they ran around a lot. But unlike the last two, this pair obviously knew what they were doing. They ran cables all over the place and tapped away at their laptop. They rang the office a lot, but instead of saying 'What ve do next?', this pair were saying things like 'No problem Boss. SNR of 23 and climbing'. They oozed confidence and optimism. They banged a new pole on the side of the house, which is going to annoy the neighbours, but they are the only people who will see it.

They have left now. They were thorough gentlemen. They were horrified at the way I had been treated by the last lot. They have left me with a better connection than I have ever had before.

So it does pay to be an old grouch. It does pay to complain. It does pay to be a right pain in the backside. But you can only do these things if you are old and experienced like me.

I can relax now and return to my favourite pastime – ~~porn~~ Google Earth.

NOW IT'S THE HEALTH NAZIS WHO ARE AFTER ME

I have been a pipe-smoker all my life. Well, actually I think I gave it up once, somewhere around junior infants, but it didn't last long.

Other people enjoy it too. Many's the time people have said how they like the smell of pipe smoke. Unless of course I have run out of tobacco and am smoking tea leaves, in which case they moan a bit.

A few years ago, the pub in our village was repainted. The smell of paint was terrible for about a week. They pleaded with me to sit there and smoke away because I masked the smell. (I presume they meant the pipe, not me personally.) Free pints for a week. Who says smoking is unhealthy?

Then the Health Nazis came along.

First I wasn't allowed smoke in the office. No problem. It gave me a chance to slope off every ten minutes. Genuine excuse – 'Goin' for a smoke, Boss'.

Then the real killer came – no more smoking in pubs. Now that was mean and vicious. I had to give up the drink.

And I enjoy my pint. No one asked for this ban. It was dumped on us by a minister because he wanted to be smug in Brussels and do something they hadn't asked for either ('look how progressive we are in Ireland').

I know I'm going to get a lot of do-gooders here saying that smoking is unhealthy and we must think of the staff and other customers and secondary smoking. Rubbish. Most of the crowds outside the pubs these nights are the staff having a quick puff. And if you like fresh air so much, then go sup your pint on the top of a mountain. Or if you are so worried about the state of your health, then give up alcohol. It's bad for you.

If I do want a pint now, I either have to sit in the pub and suffer the stench of air freshener, stale drink, bodily wind and the odd waft from the toilets, or I have to sit outside and freeze among the used kegs. And they wonder why the pub trade is falling off.

But now I have seen the latest thing the Health Nazis have produced.

They have invented a device that detects a cigarette being lit! Now, if they invented a device that detected a paedophile unzipping his trousers, then that would be something. But this is ridiculous. I can just see them sitting in their control room waiting for some poor bastard to light up so that they can go down and beat him to a pulp (but it's for his own good of course).

I quote from their blurb – 'Our STEALTH smoking detectors are truly unique devices. This is truly innovative technology where the device is not really a cigarette smoke detector but more of a cigarette smoker detector.'

Or worse – 'Our high tech system(s) actually transmit the alarm via a wireless transmitter to an intelligent receiver that determines which bathroom or area is signalling and in turn transmits a coded pager message that 'someone lit up in bathroom number 16' and the enforcer or his delegate can take immediate action and visit the bathroom where the infraction has occurred. The smoker is amazed that somehow he got caught! What a beautiful thing!'

And a footnote to their blurb – 'We're the company with the sunny disposition.' Wrong! You are the company with sanctimonious smug disposition.

As a matter of interest, what is wrong with smoking in the toilet? Are they worried about passive smoking there? Where I come from, people do not linger in toilets, unless they are up to no good (or are having a quiet smoke). And when do you go into a toilet, what are you breathing anyway? I'll tell you. Aromas that have originated *inside* other people. Lovely!

Give me tobacco smoke every time.

ONLY SPAMMERS NEED APPLY

I am going to open a university. It is going to offer the usual range of qualifications, from certificates up to, and including, Masters degrees. But before you go rushing off to apply, there is one thing you should know – it is a very exclusive university. To qualify for entry, you must be a spammer.

I receive a lot of spam. Don't we all? And the one thing that seems to be lacking in all spammers is a basic education. They can't spell. They haven't even the basic rudiments of grammar. They don't seem to realise that it undermines their message.

For example, I defy you to invest in a company that advertises:

> We're glad to present a new suggestion you won't deny. Here is a great chance to make money without running the risk of losing them. Without doubt, it is a firm bargain.

Can you imagine holding erudite and profound conversations with a life-long partner who introduces herself (or himself?) with the following:

> Hi there lovely,
>
> I was searching the net few days ago. I am new to this thing and saw your profile. I decided to email you cause I found you attractive. I might come down to your city in few weeks. Let me know if we can meet each other in person.
>
> I am attractive girl. I am sure you won't regret it.

Would you buy Viagra or Cialis from 'VjAGRA_nw_$1,78, CjALiS_uz_$3,00' when they can't even spell it? The one that finally gave me the idea was a gem I received the other day –

> Hello Rgjournal!!.
>
> Absloutely are no cotnracted tests, classes, books, or interviews !
> Attain a_Bachelor,s Masters., MBA, and Doctorate

> (PhD) diploma.
> Get the rewards nad support_that comes with a.diploma !
>
> Nobody is reejcted
> anonymityq uestionless

Even the universities need educating!

So my friend Sam is going to set up my mail system, so that every spam will receive a reply:

> Deer Spammer
>
> We thank your for message I red, adn we hav offer you can refuse not. I can help you impres your reeders by edyoucating you in how to spelling and make words put together.
>
> You wil get gooder sales. You wil sell things better. Aply now to the Headrambles University! You wil regret it not.
>
> Replie to this male with your (no doubt, stolen) credit card detales.
>
> Yoors sinseerly
>
> Grandad

DEAR SANTA

Dear Santa,

You may remember me. I wrote to you somewhere around the middle of the last century asking for an electric train set. I must have been bold that year because I got a pair of socks instead. I didn't mind because they were probably more useful. I used them to keep my toy cars in.

I did lose faith in you after that for a few decades, and I'm sorry.

Now I'm entering my second childhood, so I can believe in you again. So I'm giving you another chance. I have been very good for the last year, and I'm not going to ask for anything as complicated as an electric train set (though I would still like one sometime).

I'm not going to ask for anything like World Peace. I'll leave that to beauty queens and Rose of Tralee contestants. I just want simple things.

Firstly I'd like a set of marbles. Herself keeps telling me I'm losing mine, so I'd better have some new ones.

Talking of simple things, could you please give George W. a few more brain cells? Just enough to let him work out for himself that he's an idiot. And teach him to make love, not war.

Could you please remove all the speed bumps on the roads I use? That's not asking too much surely? I'm tired of my head banging off the car roof every time I go over one.

And talking of roads, could you please remove all that paint they keep putting on roads? All those lanes and arrows and warnings just confuse me, and I'm afraid I might cause an accident because I keep finding myself in the wrong lane.

I suppose there is no chance of having my old teeth back? Preferably the ones I had before 1971 when that nasty accident knocked all my good ones out? The ones I have now are OK but they're not quite the same thing.

I'd like a new government too, please. Not a change of government, but a brand new one. One that cares about the people and not themselves. One that will line my pockets, not their own.

Could you please help all those people who are obsessed with sport and find them something else to do? Like reading or sleeping?

And if you do find yourself with a spare electric train set, I still haven't lost hope …

Lovingly yours,
Grandad.

P.S. I'm sure the children of the world would enjoy toys for much longer if they didn't have batteries and remote controls. On second thoughts, could you make it so that all children require batteries and remote controls?

SMOKING IN OFFICES IS GOOD FOR BUSINESS

Many years ago, I worked in Dublin in a nasty modern office block. It was a horrible place. The windows faced south so it got *very* hot in summer, but we couldn't open the windows because of the noise and fumes from the street below.

However, the lads in the Support Department found a use for all this sunlight. They went into horticulture in a very big way. So big, that the room became quite dark.

Incidentally, I should point out that the window in question looked out onto one of Dublin's biggest garda stations.

Now the plants loved it there and they flourished. The other staff (the innocent ones) became quite jealous. One girl asked if she could bring one home. So they gave her a fine specimen. She brought it home on the bus, all the way out to Leixlip. I'd love to know what the other passengers thought.

Of course we had a fine time every lunch hour. This was long before the stupid 'no smoking in offices' rule and we made the most of it. Come two o'clock, most of us didn't know where we were, and we certainly didn't care. The Support Department at this stage had vanished in a blue haze, and the smell permeated the entire floor of the building. Somehow, nobody outside the room seemed to notice. They were all probably smashed as well.

Naturally, when the public rang in with their complaints after lunch, they would get weird and wonderful replies from the lads. I remember when one unfortunate woman got frustrated and demanded the name of a manager. 'Ron Atkinson' says the lad before hanging up. Another complained that she thought some electrical equipment was 'live'. So the lads told her to feed it.

Sadly all good things must come to an end. One day one of the secretaries came in and asked if they could have a couple of plants for the public reception desk. It was after lunch so the lads weren't exactly thinking straight, and they told her to go ahead.

It was a magnificent polished oak counter. The secretary was right – the plants looked lovely there, resplendent at each end. Then some damned member of the public had to come in and ask why there were two marijuana plants on the counter.

There was mayhem for a couple of days and the plants disappeared (I never discovered who robbed them, but it wasn't me). Heads rolled (the last thing to be rolled that summer!), one was sacked and one or two ended up with severe cautions. The rest of us ended up with withdrawals.

After that, the lads lost heart. They became depressed and took it out on the customers. I think the customers missed the inventive replies they used to get too. They started to complain that the lads weren't so helpful. Lunch hour was never the same again.

WITHIN EASY COMMUTING DISTANCE OF DUBLIN

The first thing you have to learn if you are buying a house in Ireland is that you are going to have to commute. Every house ad in the paper says 'within commuting distance of Dublin'. This is true, because the commuter belt for Dublin now covers the entire country. So if you are selling a cowshed in Clifden, Schull or Glenties, you can now say it is 'within commuting distance of Dublin'. But you must not confuse 'commuting distance' with 'commuting time'. They are slightly different.

Now just about anywhere in Ireland is within 250 miles of Dublin. So at an average speed of fifty miles per hour, you'll make it in five hours. That is plenty. You get up at three in the morning, do what has to be done, and hit the road. You'll be at your desk by nine. You leave at half five, get home by half ten, have your dinner, be introduced to your children (who have forgotten who you are) and will be in bed by twelve. This gives you a whole three hours sleep, which is enough for anyone.

What they don't mention is that the roads are just a tad crowded. Only a little bit mind, but enough.

So you get up at three, hit the road by four and reach the Red Cow roundabout by half eight. If it is a good day (for example, mid August when the schools are on holidays and most people are abroad) you will only take a further two hours to reach the office. So you arrive at your desk at half ten and now have to make up time. So you don't leave your office until half seven. It takes you another two hours to reach the Red Cow roundabout, so you finally hit the open road at half nine. And the chances are it *will* be the open road. They love digging up roads here and leaving temporary traffic lights. So that'll add another hour or two to your journey. So you get home at three, just in time to leave again. But if the weather is bad and it's a Monday evening, you'll just about get as far as Kinnegad before you have to turn around and start Tuesday's commute.

So the main trunk roads are crowded each evening with commuters dashing to see how near they can get to their homes before turning around again. There is a rumour that one bloke in a souped-up car once got as far as Sligo before having to turn around again. I don't believe it though.

So. If you are out and about at around three in the

morning somewhere in the wilds of the Irish countryside, and you see a tired looking bedraggled motorist doing a three-point turn in the road, give him a smile. Give him a wave. He needs cheering up. He has just finished one day's work, and is starting on the next.

MORE SPAMS, AND MY REPLY

As you may gather, I love spam. It is a source of endless amusement. I received this one today. Seeing as she is a philanthropist, I have to answer it.

> From: DR.JULIET BLINK (Philanthropist)
>
> Dear good friend,
>
> Subject Matter: SINCERE COMPENSATION.
>
> You might find it so difficult to remember me. Though, it is indeed, a very long time. On my singular, I am much delighted and privileged to contact you again, after couple of years now. It takes fate, courage and God's fearing to remember old friends and at the same time, to show gratification to them, despite circumstances that made things, not worked out as we projected then.
>
> I take this liberty to inform you that, the transaction we were pursing together, finally worked out by God's infinite mercy and I decided to contact you, just to let you know. I have conscience as a human begin, due to your tremendous effort and contribution to make things work out in retrospect.

Meanwhile, I must inform you that, I am presently in Luxemburg for numerous business negotiations and establishment. I just arrived yesterday night and checked inn, in a hotel and decided to go down to the hotel business centre to mail you. Now, with my sincere heart, I have raised and signed an International Cashier's Bank Draft, to the tune of USD $520,000.00 (FIVE HUNDRED AND TWENTY THOUSAND DECIMAL ZERO-ZERO UNITED STATES DOLLARS) only in your name as COMPENSATION to your dedication, humanity and contribution, as it were.

Please, contact NOW, my confidential secretary, she is in the name of:

MR WOOD WILLAMS (Secretary)

Email: xxxxxxxx@xxxxxx.xxx

Tel.: +000000000000

You are to forward to her, the following:

1. YOUR FULL NAME & ADDRESS

2. YOUR TELEPHONE NUMBER (If necessary)

She will advise you further about the shipment of the ICBD to your Residence Address or Office Address you may provided. Feel free to reach via this very mail address. Most importantly, the ICBD has only validity period of 12 banking days.

So, your early response to that effect, shall be admired. You have to mind the days on route shipment.

Sincerely Yours,

Dr.JULIET BLINK. (Philanthropist)

So here is my reply

Dear good friend, – Hold on now! I'm sure with a name like Blink, I'd remember you if you were a friend.

Subject Matter: SINCERE COMPENSATION. – What is Sincere Compensation? Or, come to that, what is insincere compensation?

You might find it so difficult to remember me. Though, it is indeed, a very long time. On my singular, I am much delighted and privileged to contact you again, after couple of years now. – Yes. I do find it difficult to remember you, because we never met. Not even a couple of years ago. However, on my bicycle, I'm glad you are privileged.

It takes fate, courage and God's fearing to remember old friends and at the same time, to show gratification to them, despite circumstances that made things, not worked out as we projected then. – Actually, I find an address book is easier.

I take this liberty to inform you that, the transaction we were pursing together, finally worked out by God's infinite mercy and I decided to contact you, just to let you know. I have conscience as a human begin, due to your tremendous effort and contribution to make things work out in retrospect. – I'm glad things worked out, but I don't remember pursuing anything. And what's this thing about being a 'human begin'? Are you the missing link?

Meanwhile, I must inform you that, I am presently in Luxemburg for numerous business negotiations and establishment. I just arrived yesterday night *and checked inn, in a hotel and decided to go down to the hotel business centre to mail you. Now, with my sincere heart, I have raised and signed an International Cashier's Bank Draft, to the tune of USD $520,000.00 (FIVE HUNDRED AND TWENTY THOUSAND DECIMAL ZERO-ZERO UNITED STATES DOLLARS) only in your name as COMPENSATION to your dedication, humanity and contribution, as it were.* – I hope you are enjoying your stay in Luxemburg, though I'm not sure whether you are staying at an Inn or a Hotel. Wow! That's a lot of money, though you needn't have spelled it out. I believe you. It'll come in handy. I take it this is for my blogging efforts? Though I'm not sure I like the 'as it were' bit. That sounds a bit sarcastic.

Please, contact NOW, my confidential secretary, she is in the name of:

MR WOOD WILLAMS (Secretary) – I take it Mr Williams hasn't had the operation yet? Or is he lying about his gender?

You are to forward to her, the following:

1. YOUR FULL NAME & ADDRESS

2. YOUR TELEPHONE NUMBER (If necessary)
– There you go again! Your secretary is a MAN. Look under the desk if you don't believe me. And how do I know if my number is necessary?

She will advise you further about the shipment of the ICBD to your Residence Address or Office Address you may provided. Feel free to reach via this very mail address. Most importantly, the ICBD has only validity period of 12 banking days. – Now look here! I'm getting tired of telling you this; he's a man. Ask him to take down his trousers. I'm sure he'll oblige. And be careful. Your grammar is beginning to break up a bit. Are you driving through a tunnel?

So, your early response to that effect, shall be admired. You have to mind the days on route shipment. – What?

Sincerely Yours,

Grandad (Aged Philanthropist and Blogger).

THE SWEET SMELL OF SUCCESS

I don't know if it's my age or what, but I am becoming more intolerant of some smells.

There are some smells that I love – freshly cut grass, fried onions, honeysuckle (or woodbine or Lonicera or whatever-you-want-to-call-it). The world is full of wonderful natural scents.

The smells that I have come to hate are the artificial ones. Any smell that comes out of a can or bottle drives me mad. It gives me a headache. My eyes water. My nose stings. I was going to say man-made smells, but frankly I would prefer BO to perfume or aftershave.

When they brought in that 'no-smoking-in-pubs' crap, our local started using air freshener by the bucket load. They must have done some deal with a cheap factory in the Far East and imported tanker loads of the stuff. I couldn't go in any more. Even walking past the place gave me a headache.

Even before the ban, I'd go to the gents, and no sooner would I start to do what I had to do than the air freshener thingy on the wall would give a little psssst. I'd have to run out. I nearly got done a couple of times for indecency.

They have ads on the telly. One shows a room in black and white. Then a woman comes in and plugs in an air freshener, and the room fills with colour. Birds, flowers and butterflies magically appear. What are they on? I'd be out of that room like greased lightning.

Herself is a sucker for the advertising. She gets the idea that sticking a yoke in a socket is going to bring peace, harmony, tranquillity and beauty to a room. As soon as I sniff it (I can usually detect it as soon as she gets in the car from the shops), I throw it at the nearest passing tourist. The daft thing is that she hates artificial stinks too. I'll never understand women and shopping.

It's only the artificial ones that do it. I can stand all day by a field where they are spreading slurry. I can tolerate a lift full of flatulence (usually my own). Rubbish bins hold no terrors. I don't necessarily *like* them, but I can take them at a pinch. But give me one whiff of aftershave, deodorant, air freshener, perfume or anything scented, and I'm gone.

I was talking to a neighbour about this and she agreed with me. She said she'd rather the smell of old socks to air freshener.

So I am opening a new business. I am going to soak my old socks during their monthly wash and throw in my runners for good measure. Then I'm going to bottle the water. I'll distil it a bit, and maybe add a drop or two of underarm. It should be quite pungent.

But it will be natural.

OUR COUNCIL HAS GONE ROUND THE BEND

There is a lovely valley near me. A river meanders along it and a road follows the bank of the river.

So the road meanders a bit too. It's a lovely road. There are mossy walls on one side and the river on the other. It is a heavily wooded valley, and the colours are beautiful at any time of year.

As I said, it's a very twisty road with lots of bends (actually, it's difficult to have a twisty road *without* bends, now that I think of it). It is difficult to drive there at more than about thirty (or fifty, in new money), and for some of the bends, you have to go a lot slower than that.

Our local council, in their infinite wisdom have decreed that this road has a limit of fifty (or eighty in new money), which is much too high. Now this is stupid and all the locals know it. But in fairness to the council there are loads of signs warning about not overtaking (you couldn't anyway) and dangerous bends and more bends. There are more warning signs than bends. There are even signs warning of deer, but I've never seen one there.

Yet there are some prats out there who think that a limit sign means that that is the speed you have to use. So they try barrelling along at fifty. And they come unstuck on the bends. So there are always dozens of hubcaps lying around, where they have hit the footpath. Serves 'em right. But a couple of years ago, there was a fatality there. A car went into the river. I don't know how that was physically possible if the signs were observed, but it happened.

The council have now decided to straighten the road. This is impossible, because there is a river on one side, and the side of the valley on the other. They are trying anyway. So far, they have succeeded in hacking down a lot of the lovely trees and have removed most of the mossy wall. They have put up great big concrete walls instead and are covering them in granite. It must be costing a fortune.

But the bends aren't much better. In fact they have managed to introduce one or two more. And I'll guarantee that when the work is finished and they have destroyed the look of the place (at great cost), they will put up a lower speed limit.

Now, why didn't they just do that in the first place?

GREETINGS TO THE CIA

I would like to extend a very Happy Holiday to my friends at the CIA. I know you have been keeping a very careful lookout for me for the last few months. The black van outside with the dark windows and the satellite dish on the roof is very reassuring. I haven't had any break-ins since it arrived (apart of course from the lads, but they have to be able to plant their bugs. Don't they?).

I'm still not quite clear whether you are watching me because I have a thing against George W., or whether you are protecting me because you see me as the Voice of Hope for America.

Is there any truth in the rumour that George W. is going to rename the months of the year after himself and his family? I also believe he is writing his thoughts and philosophies on the back of a matchbox, and that everyone will have to learn it as well as the Declaration of Independence and the Constitution?

I won't ask you to pass on a message to him from me. It would be too rude, and physically very difficult for him to achieve.

Please don't launch a surface to air attack on Santa when he flies in. It would be too hard to explain to the grandchildren. I'll bring some mince pies out to the lads in the van, or they are welcome to call in. It must be freezing out there.

They'll have to drink Guinness though as I don't approve of Budweiser (or Bud as you call it).

Anyway, I hope you have a peaceful holiday (I know you don't like calling it Christmas).

Grandad.

THERE IS NO LIGHT AT THE END OF THE TUNNEL

To those of you who have not been watching the news, or reading the papers, Bertie's Hole is now open. Bertie's Hole is a new tunnel that links the port, in the centre of Dublin with the ring motorway. The idea is to remove heavy lorries from our city streets. So far, so good.

We'll ignore the trivial little problems, like the fact that it isn't high enough to take the bigger lorries, or that it floods. We will look at the logistics.

In their wisdom, the planners drove the tunnel north to link up with the M1 and then the M50 (the ring road). There is only one major city to the north of Dublin and that is Belfast. The other major cites, like Galway, Limerick, Cork, Waterford and Wexford all lie to the west, south-west and south.

So any lorry heading for (say) Cork, has to head north until it reaches the ring road and then head anti-clockwise all the way around the city to reach the Cork road. This is a distance of 16 miles, and it includes an expensive toll bridge and a major stretch of motorway that is being rebuilt. In other words, it is very slow and very expensive.

The alternative is to take the direct route through the city, along the quays, which involves a bit of traffic, but you miss out on the roadworks and the toll bridge. That is a distance of 7 miles. If you are heading south to Waterford or Wexford, the difference in the distances is a lot worse.

Which route would you take? Which route do you think the lorries are taking? And the city planners are completely baffled as to why the lorries aren't using Bertie's Hole.

> But we built yiz a lovely tunnel. It cost us €750,000,000. Why aren't you using it? The fellas going to Belfast say it's great, but the rest of yiz keep driving through the city. Why?

And the truckers reply with their usual eloquence:

> Fuck off. We don't like the extra distance or the tolls or the motorway delays!

So the Irish government does what it always does – it passes a law. From 19 February, it will be illegal to drive a lorry through the city. That is when the fun begins.

ALL I WANT FOR CHRISTMAS

Why do people buy so much food for Christmas? I guarantee that if you stand in any shopping centre car park on 23 December you will see people pushing trolleys laden down with bread, milk, toilet rolls and other essentials.

Nothing wrong with that? But they will have stocked up for a month at least. Who on earth is going to use ten loaves of bread in one day? Who is going to drink five gallons of milk? And is their cooking so bad that they are going to need twenty rolls of toilet paper in one day?

The shops are open on Christmas Eve. They will all be open again two days later, if not sooner. There are mini-markets in petrol stations that are open on Christmas Day. So why all this panic buying?

The last time I did my Christmas shopping in a supermarket, a few years ago, I swore I would never do it again. I had to circle the car park for half an hour before getting a space. Then I found that people were literally fighting to get trolleys. They were stalking shoppers as they came out of the shop and grabbing their trolleys virtually before they were empty.

Then I got inside. Oh God! It took two hours of battling through jammed lanes. People with two trolleys each. The entire town seemed to be in there.

Then it came to checkout time. Another hour and a half of queuing! I am not joking. The queues were literally the length of the shop. Staff were wandering up and down wearing Santy hats and handing out sweets to us to try to prevent a riot. I got to intimately know the price of every single item in the lane I was in. And then of course, I had to fight to hold onto my trolley outside until I had unloaded it, as there were ten irate people trying to grab it off me.

Never again.

So what is it all about? They are buying enough food to last at least a month. Why? Why not just buy for a couple of days and come back after Christmas when the shops are quiet?

And of course there is The Drink. Crates of beer. I have seen a family loading their car with three trolley loads of beer. I remember one year I was behind some woman. She had a trolley that was groaning under the weight of drink. Gallons of beer and crates of whiskey. There was a child buried under it somewhere. She got to the checkout and I had to laugh. I quote: 'Bless ya luv. I'll pay for de drink, but could ya spare an old loaf a bread for de child?'

Now I do my shopping on the Internet. He's due to deliver in a couple of hours. I had to book the delivery slot weeks ago. I ordered a bit more than usual, but that is because we have a bit of a houseful on Christmas Day. So there are a couple of extra cartons of milk, and a few cans of beer for the guests. And of course there is the turkey and ham. Apart from that it isn't much more than a normal shop.

After all, the shops will all be open on the day after Christmas.

NEW TRAFFIC SYSTEM COMING TO IRELAND

In the run up to the next general election, the government has announced a new initiative to bring Ireland in line with our European partners. The following is the essence of the announcement made this morning:

For centuries, Ireland has been the poor relation of England. We inherited their laws, their architecture, their language and their way of life. We see ourselves now as an independent state that is more European than British. We have adopted the euro as our currency. We have established Irish as an official language within the European Union. We have won the Eurovision Song Contest more times than anyone else. It is time for the next step.

We propose that from the 1 July 2007, we will adopt the European standard of driving on the right hand side of the road. This is a major initiative that will bring us in line with the rest of Europe, along with metrication. Furthermore, with the rate of immigration expected to increase, by the year 2010, the majority of the population will have originated in countries that drive on the right. We already have the physical infrastructure in place. It is just a matter of public education.

Starting from the 1 February, motorists will have a five-month period in which to have their vehicles adapted to left-hand drive. During this period, road signs and traffic lights will also be adapted. All new vehicles sold after this date will be configured for left-hand drive.

Starting on the 1 July, there will be a period of transition. Initially, all buses and articulated vehicles will move to the right to allow for a period of adjustment. Car owners may opt to make the switch themselves on an individual basis, depending on their level of confidence.

Starting on the 1 August, all motorists outside city limits will be required to drive on the right. And finally on the 1 September, all city traffic will make the transition.

It is appreciated that there will be some confusion initially, but death rates within the first year are expected to be below the 50,000 mark. This is a small price to pay for the estimated five lives a year that will be saved after the transition.

The government is committed to reducing the appalling death rate on our roads, and to further harmonisation with our European neighbours.

FOUNDATIONS LAID FOR NEW CITY

I went down to our local planning office a couple of months ago. There was a very friendly girl behind the counter. She took my plans and offered to go through them to make sure

I was submitting all the right documents. She went through all the plans and the elevations and the cross-sections. She went through the documentation. She looked happy enough. Then she came to the location plan.

'This can't be right,' says she.

'What's wrong?' says I.

'You are applying for planning permission for a marina, with facilities to upgrade to a full harbour, but it's miles from the sea!'

'That's right.'

'And it's half way up a mountain. Are you mad?'

'Yes,' says I, 'but surely that has nothing to do with the application?'

So she accepted it. The notices were posted. Nobody objected. I got my permission. Because they all knew I was mad. Construction starts next year.

And shortly after that global warming will start to melt the polar icecaps. Not to mention the Greenland icecap. Sea levels are going to rise. I'm living on the side of a valley a long way from the sea (the planning office got that right), but in a hundred years or so, my little mountainside retreat will be on the shoreline of the new sea level.

Now, when the sea levels rise, all the cities will be underwater, and most of the towns too. Everyone will be taking to the high ground. They'll need port facilities. They'll build a new city around my harbour. They'll call the city Portgrandad.

I won't be around for any of this, but my great-grandchildren will be lords and masters of all they survey. I'll be hailed as the Great Visionary. I may be mad, but I'm not stupid.

WANTED - TRANSLATOR FOR CORNER SHOP

I was in the village yesterday, and I picked up one of those night classes brochures. You never know. They might be holding classes in something interesting like *macramé* or flower-arranging.

There were the usual courses. There was life drawing, but Herself said no to that one. There was pottery, belly-dancing, golf, bridge and cooking. There were a few strange ones, like hair extension technician, angel meditation and Stott pilates (that sounds like a Brazilian footballer).

There was one I mused over – Blogging for Beginners. I decided I wasn't ready for that yet. But what really struck me was the number of foreign language courses. They have French, German, Italian, Japanese, Polish, Spanish and Russian. I can understand the likes of French and Spanish, as it's handy to have the language when on holiday. But Russian and Polish?

Then it struck me. What they are doing is teaching us foreign languages so we can go into our local shops and speak to the staff! More and more, I am encountering Manuel from *Fawlty Towers*. I go into a shop and ask for pipe cleaners or something and all I get is *que?* or a blank stare.

I like immigrants. They add colour and diversity to a gene pool. But I do wish they'd learn the language. Particularly before getting a job that deals with the public. I mean to say, what is the point of shouting a few choice swear words at the chap in the call centre if he doesn't understand what you are saying? I am dreading the day they employ a foreigner in the chemist. If ever you need to be able to communicate, then that's it. I visualise the scene where I go in for Xanax and come out with Durex.

So now we need to learn their language rather than the other way around. I have only one thing to say to that.

Póg mo thóin

A ROUGH GUIDE TO IRELAND FOR AMERICANS

Ireland is an island situated in the Atlantic between Newfoundland and the Isle of Man. It is 300 miles long (I learned that in school), whereas America is only 7 inches wide (I just measured it on a National Geographic map and they must be right).

It has an Atlantic climate, which means the winters are mild and wet. In contrast, the summers are mild and wet. Occasionally we have three consecutive days when the sun shines. We call that a 'heat wave'. When we have a heat wave, we walk around semi-naked and complain about the awful heat. The rest of the time we wear overcoats and moan about the cold (and how we never have heat waves).

We are a democracy, where every few years we elect the same set of gougers (roughly equivalent to Republicans) to power. We also have a president who is usually called Mary. She lives in her Áras in a public park in the capital city, Dublin.

The Irish have three main cities – Dublin, Cork and Boston MA.

There are two official languages in Ireland – English and Irish. Irish used to be the second language, but recently due to an incredible influx of immigrants, it has slipped to 145th place. It is still however an official language of the European Union. Its primary function these days is to confuse visitors to the country.

Ireland is a peaceful and friendly country (and we will fight anyone who says otherwise). We have the only navy and air force in the world where they go home for dinner. We have a largish army who spend their time abroad trying to keep the peace. They get shot at a lot, but aren't allowed to shoot back.

We adopted the euro as our currency in 2001 just to piss off the British, who stubbornly refuse to adopt it. We have outdone the US in that we have banned smoking everywhere except in the street or at home. All Irish smokers are now agoraphobic. Guns are illegal here, unless you are a member of a drugs gang, or you're a paramilitary in which case they are mandatory. We drive on the left, except at pub closing time. Then you can drive whichever side of the road you like. Contrary to popular belief, no one here wears Aran sweaters. We only produce them to sell to gullible Americans.

Ireland has won the Eurovision Song Contest so many times that we are now shunned by the rest of Europe and they gang up on us and won't let us win again. Which is just as well because the standard is now crap.

Our national drinks are whiskey and Guinness. Irish whiskey is not to be confused with Scotch whisky (note the difference in spelling), which is an inferior product. I won't even try to compare it to American whiskey, which is equivalent to turpentine.

The Irish have a great sense of humour. We prove this by constantly electing Bertie Ahern as our leader.

Last year we had a population of around three million. This year we have a population of around four million. This is because Europeans think that this is the Land of Milk and Honey, and they all want to live here. Ireland is an extremely wealthy country. The only problem is that the government insists on holding on to all our cash, so the people are relatively poor and can't afford to buy their own houses, which are stupidly expensive.

Irish history is confusing and contentious. It has been written by two nations – the British and Irish. Neither can agree as to what happened, so we generally just ignore it except to have parades from time to time. Anyway American history only goes back a couple of hundred years, so you don't have that much to learn. Ours goes back over 6,000 years, which is a heck of a lot of history for a schoolchild to cope with. If you want to know more about Ireland, then read my blog.

Oh, and by the way – we do have snakes, but we call them politicians.

REAL REALITY TELEVISION

Will someone please tell me what this reality television is all about? As far as I can make out, and correct me if I'm wrong, they get a gang of extremely low IQ people with personalities that are bound to clash and they lock them in a house. And before anyone says that they have seen high IQ people in there, I would say that no intelligent person would want to subject themselves to that.

We are then meant to sit back and watch them live their lives. Why? What is the fascination? Why not just put a few flies and a couple of spiders in a jam jar and watch them?

The organisers of these programmes know what they are at. You can just see their minds working.

'OK now, we have a mild mannered person here from India. Let's stick in someone from the National Front. That should get the sparks flying!' The organisers then throw their hands up in horror when the blood starts to flow. But it is *exactly* what they wanted. Front-page news. Everyone tuning in to see what the fuss is about. They've hit the headlines.

What is the attraction of this? I couldn't give a flying fuck about them. Why should I care if some bimbo is in tears because someone looked sideways at her? Why should I care that someone is being asked to eat live slugs marinated in pig poo? They knew what they were letting themselves in for when they signed up.

There are obviously enough sad people out there who want to submit themselves to public humiliation, so why not stick them all in a disused hangar in the middle of nowhere. We can *tell* them that there are cameras watching them (but of course there aren't), and just leave them there to fight it out. They'll be happy, and the rest of us can get on with our lives.

Or why not at least make it interesting? I would suggest that we take these contestants and ship them to an African wildlife park. Loads of cameras, but no one in the background with guns. This is reality after all. The bimbos and airheads get their moment of glory in the sun, and the animals get fed.

I could watch that.

COULD YOU ANSWER A FEW QUESTIONS PLEASE?

I used to be plagued by cold-callers on the phone. They were all trying to sell me something I didn't want. The worst offender was Smart Telecom, trying to get me to switch my phone account to them.

'You won't regret it,' says they. Ha ha! How wrong they would have been. (For the benefit of overseas readers, Smart failed to pay their bills and left thousands of their customers high and dry with no phones.)

Lately I've come across a new breed of cold-callers. The surveys. I keep getting calls from people who hastily tell me that they don't want to sell me anything, but could I answer a few questions for a survey please.

The first couple I let through and answered their questions. Then it occurred to me – why not have some fun? I didn't ask them to ring after all. So the next few that came on, I answered their questions with random answers.

How many bottles of water do you drink in a day? – 156.

How many children under the age of 18 reside with you? – 25.

What type of pet do you have? – A bottlenose dolphin.

How far do you commute to work? – 15 feet.

You get the idea.

I think they began to get suspicious, because the calls started to tail off a bit. This annoyed me because I was having fun. So I decided to go for broke.

The phone rang the other night.

'Hello. Please-don't-hang-up-I-am-not-trying-to-sell-you-anything.'

'Is this a survey?' says I.

'Yes,' says he, sounding very relieved. 'I won't take up much of your time. I just want to ask some quick questions.'

'No problem,' says I. 'Can I see some identification?'

Long pause.

'Pardon?' says he.

'I'll need to see some identification so that I know you are who you say you are.'

'But I only want to ask you some general questions. No personal ones.'

'Ah!' says I, 'but if a stranger arrived at your door and didn't identify himself, would you invite him in even if he said he wasn't going to steal anything?'

He thought for a while. 'No. Probably not.'

'Damn sure, you wouldn't,' says I. 'Now show me some identification.'

'I can't. This is a phone line. I take it you don't want to take the survey?'

'I don't mind answering any and all of your questions, if you show me some identification first.'

There was a very long pause. He muttered something and hung up.

Now a lot of companies get their information this way. And then they throw it back at us in their advertising. So the next time you see an ad on television proudly announcing that: '99% of all known cats brush their teeth with Gromore', don't mind it. It was just me having fun.

PLEASE HOLD THE LINE FOR TWO WEEKS

I just rang my broadband company again for the laugh. I am supposed to be getting an upgrade to my service for the last while. So I took a stiff shot of whiskey and phoned them.

Their phone system of course uses a voice processing unit. Apparently that is what they call that bloody irritating 'press 1 for giblets, press 2 for knob rot' thingy that drives me mad. I pressed my buttons and waited.

A pleasant recorded voice tells me that due to the volume of calls, I should be answered within two minutes. Ten minutes later, the phone is answered.

He said something that I couldn't understand (my Swahili isn't that fluent), but I thought I heard something about a number. So I gave him my account number. He rattled off my name and address, which I understood, and it was reassuring because it meant that that part of their system was working anyway.

'What is the nature of the problem?' says he.

'Nothing,' says I. 'I'm just phoning to see if there is any sign of my upgrade.'

This confused him a bit. He had a customer who didn't

have a problem and that obviously didn't appear on his screen prompting system. He muttered something (I'm not sure if it was in Urdu or Hindustani) and started typing. I have never heard so much typing. Either I caught him in the middle of writing his autobiography, or else he was reprogramming the system to accept problems from people who don't have a problem.

Then the phone went dead. I waited, because I had nothing better to do. There was a long silence. Then suddenly he was back. Still typing.

'I'm sorry,' says he, 'can I put you on hold?'

'No problem,' says I, as I poured another whiskey.

They played the usual musak at me for a while, and then he came back.

'We are upgrading people in rotation. We have not done your area yet.'

'I know that,' says I, 'but have you any idea when it might be done?'

'We estimate within two to three weeks,' says he.

'I phoned on the first of October last year and I was told two to three weeks then,' says I.

'We estimate within two to three weeks,' says he.

I thanked him and hung up. Two seconds later, I got an email saying that a Support Ticket had been opened.

'Great,' thinks I, 'at least they have a record of my call.'

One second later I got an email saying that my Support Ticket had been closed. I'll phone them again in May.

COME ON IRELAND - WAKE UP

It's funny how blogging tends to focus the mind. I didn't know it would actually change the way I perceive the world, but it has. It has also taught me a few things about the world. I am about to make a momentous statement. One that I never before thought I would make: *Americans (in general) are not stupid.*

There. I said it. I actually feel a bit better now.

Americans are just different. I don't like the way they talk with their 'Hey Guys' and their 'take a raincheck' and weird expressions like that, but that's their business. I also don't like the way they mis-spell everything and abbreviate everything. They even abbreviate their cities to LA and AC and the like. (If anyone is interested, I was born in D. My parents were from C and L. Herself is from L and we have lived in S, B, K and K).

Who cares if they don't know the difference between Australia and Iraq (though I hope Bush does, for the Australians' sake)? American foreign policy is a different matter, but I'll leave that for now.

The people who are stupid are the Irish!

The Irish have an obsession with America and I don't know why. The kids all have to use American slang, which drives me up the wall. They use all those irritating expressions that they have learned from *Friends* and other un-funny American TV programmes.

When she was in her 'daughter from hell' phase, our offspring used to use them all the time: 'You are soooo not right' and 'If I don't go to that party I will DIE' (she didn't know how near that last one was to the truth!).

I was parked in a car park yesterday (quite a good place to park, actually) and there was a battered old van in front of me. He had the American flag displayed in his rear window. Why? That flag appears everywhere. Why? I have seen lots of houses with basketball hoops attached to the walls, usually decorated with stars and stripes. Why? I have never seen anyone using them.

I nearly bought a new baseball bat yesterday. I don't play baseball, but I thought it might be handy if Herself got stroppy. But it had stars and stripes all over it so I didn't.

Modern children now think they are not living if they don't have a can of cola in one hand and a burger in the other at all times. They waddle around like mini Cartmans. Irish children should be reared on a diet of tripe and Guinness, like we were. And we ate at the table, not in the street (another peculiar Americanism). Another thing that drives me insane is the assumption by advertisers that if they introduce an American scenario or an American accent, that we will fall over each other to buy the product.

So my message to the people of Ireland: *You are Irish. You are not American. Think for yourselves, and don't let the television think for you. Stop being so pathetically gullible.*

BIG BROTHER IS A CONSPIRACY

The Nanny State strikes again.

So far we have had to put up with speed limits, safety helmets, seat belts, smoking bans, ban on corporal punishment and loads more. But it's all for our own good. We have to be protected from ourselves at all costs.

Now the EU and the UN have stepped in and are banning slapping for God's sake. So now we can't bring up our children without the Nanny State looking over our shoulders.

I had the living daylights walloped out of me in school on a regular basis. They even had specially made leather straps for the purpose. We behaved ourselves in class. There was respect for authority. There was no disruption in class. I didn't grow up to be a child molester or a serial killer or a thug. Mind you, there's time yet.

I gave our daughter the odd slap in the past. She deserved it. It didn't do any harm. If she was beyond reasoning, then a slap on the back of the legs worked wonders. In fact after the first couple, the threat was all that was needed. She has grown up to be a (reasonably) well-balanced person. We love her and she loves us. And she has no complaints about those slaps. (Incidentally, if there is a comment from 'offspring' denying this, then ignore it. 'Offspring' is an impostor.)

One time recently, my granddaughter started belting my grandson. She is two and he is five. But he is severely handicapped so he can't fight back. We told her to stop. We tried to distract her. She kept belting him over the head with hard toys. My daughter gave her a slap on the back of the hand. She stopped hitting her brother straight away. Lesson learned.

I give Herself the odd wallop with a baseball bat. She likes it. It shows I care. She gets me back with the frying pan when I'm dozing in the armchair. That's love.

If this law comes in and my daughter still wants to slap her children, I'm not going to stop her. It's her business, not the EUs or the UNs. They can fuck off as far as I'm concerned. Unless of course they are going to provide individual carers for each and every harassed mother who has a screaming child in the supermarket.

You know where this is leading. Don't you?

The next thing is that they will ban smoking in the home. And we won't be allowed more than one whiskey or one can of Guinness. It will all be for our own good. And we won't be allowed to fart because it upsets the ozone layer.

So to enforce all this anti-smacking, anti-smoking, anti-drinking and anti-farting, they'll have to install cameras in every room in every house. But the peasants have been brainwashed into thinking that spy-cameras are great, because of *Big Brother*.

I forecast the day will come when I reach for a top-up to my drop of whiskey and a voice will boom from the speaker in the ceiling telling me I've had enough. Or I raise the leg after a vindaloo to relieve the pressure and I get 10,000 volts up the backside because I'm producing too much methane.

When they come to install the cameras, I'll be there with Herself. We'll have the baseball bat and the frying pan handy.

NEW TUNNEL FOR CORK

Flushed with the success of the Dublin Port Tunnel, the Irish government has announced plans for an undersea link with France.

Following on the announcement that Ireland would switch to driving on the right later this year, it has been decided that this was the next logical step in the integration of our road network with the rest of Europe.

'We have the equipment now and the expertise,' said a government spokesman. 'We might as well use it.'

The tunnel will extend from Cork to the Brest Peninsula and will be a total of 470 kilometres long. It is proposed to build a service station on the Scilly Isles at the halfway point. To facilitate this, it has been agreed that Ireland will take sovereignty of the Isles in return for handing Donegal over to the Six Counties (or the Seven Counties as they will be known). This will have the added advantage of removing Daniel O'Donnell.

Asked why the tunnel wasn't being constructed between Dublin and Anglesey, which is a distance of only 80 kilometres, a government spokesman said that there wasn't that much difference in length. 'Anyway,' he continued, 'the Brits steadfastly refuse to relinquish sterling and have no intention of switching their driving sides, so they are not really part of Europe. They are really more American than European.'

When asked about travellers who wished to go from Dublin to Anglesey, he stated, 'it is only a minor detour. They can drive to France via the new tunnel, get the train through the Channel Tunnel and drive straight up to Wales. It's only a round trip of about 1,880 kilometres, and with the state of modern roads that extra is nothing. Sure I could do that in an hour or two.'

The tunnel will consist of two single-lane roads, each in

its own separate bore. In line with Port Tunnel policy, it will be insufficiently high to take large lorries.

Asked what would happen in the event of a vehicle breakdown or a slow driver, the spokesman stated that the momentum of the traffic behind the obstruction would carry it through to the far end.

'It'll be like shit flowing through a sewer,' he added.

Travellers will be asked to avoid food or drink for a period of ten hours prior to making their journey.

'We can't afford the luxury of someone stopping for a quick dump or a pee,' said the spokesman.

It is estimated that journey time will be reduced from the current eighteen hours to five hours.

'And it'll be one in the eye for those bastards in the ferry companies,' muttered the spokesman.

IN SEARCH OF LOST PUNTS

We were watching the news last night. They had an item on about lost currency.

The euro was introduced here five years ago and the old Irish pound, or punt ceased to be legal tender. You can't use it any more. It is worthless, though you can still get it changed in the Central Bank. Apparently, they estimate that there is still £300,000,000 out there. Yes – that's three hundred million punts. That is one heck of a lot of money. We started surmising where all this money could be. Under mattresses? In attics?

I casually mentioned that, now that I think of it, my father didn't trust banks, and may have buried his retirement fund under the vegetable patch. Herself never even asked why I hadn't mentioned this before. She was gone.

She came in once or twice during the evening for a drink of water and to get extra clothing. It was very cold out there, and the snow is still on the ground. She came in at around one o'clock and said she had dug the entire patch (and it's a *very* big patch) to a depth of about two feet and had found nothing.

'Ah no,' says I. 'Dad was thorough. He always said to bury something at least 3 or 4 feet down, or it might surface accidentally.'

She came in at around eight this morning and collapsed in bed. She found nothing of course, because there was nothing to find.

I've been meaning to dig that vegetable patch for ages.

WHAT WOULD THEY KNOW ANYWAY?

We were sitting by the fire last night. It was very cosy. There was a strong wind outside, so the coal fire was smoking badly which is does when the wind is from a certain direction, but we were warm and contented.

I was trying to read a book between the coughing and sneezing, and I could see Herself through the blue haze reading a magazine.

'There's a questionnaire here,' says Herself. 'It tests to see how absent-minded you are.'

So she started firing questions at me. You know the kind of thing: 'Do you ever repeat a joke or story to the same person?' (yes), or 'Do you lose items around the house?' (yes).

There were twelve questions in all. I asked her how I rated.

'I reckon you scored more than sixteen,' says Herself.

'There weren't sixteen questions,' says I.

'No,' says Herself, 'there are only twelve. That's strange.'

It turned out there was a scoring system, but she had absent-mindedly missed that. So she tried working out my score, but got confused.

'How many did you answer Yes to?' she asked.

'I've forgotten. I can't remember the questions.'

So she tried asking them again, but we got confused with the scoring system. So we dropped it. She went back to her magazine and I went back to my book and the smoke went back to filling the room.

We don't need some damned magazine trying to tell us our minds are getting old. We know our brains are as sharp as ever.

THE CURSE OF THE CENTURY

Why has our culture changed so radically in the last fifty years?

When I was young, when we weren't at school, we played outdoors. If it was raining, we played in someone's garage or garden shed. The world was one great adventure playground. We used to make our own toys. Hurling sticks became rifles, and the ultimate was a homemade soap-cart.

I grant you there wasn't as much traffic then, so we could play on the street and would only have to dodge the odd car, but that apart, the physical world is much the same.

But it is different now. You don't see many children on the streets. I haven't seen a soap-cart in decades. I haven't seen a game of marbles or a game of chasing. All I have seen is shiftless kids either hanging around aimlessly or kicking a ball around.

There is only one thing I can think of that has caused this radical change in society: *television*

There are several things wrong with television. It provides you with a means to sit and do absolutely nothing. You don't have to think. You don't have to use your imagination.

And the programmes show you a world that, in the main doesn't exist. They show you happy couples living in beautiful houses, and they all have great jobs and they are all so happy. So you begin to think to yourself 'why isn't my life like this?' Or they show you fantastic foreign scenery and tell you how wonderful it is there, and you say to yourself 'I want to be there'. In other words, television breeds discontent.

Television should be a means to tell you about the world. Instead, it has become the world. People get upset if their favourite soap character is sent to prison. They rant and rail if their favourite is voted out of *Big Brother*. They can't wait to tell you all about their favourite programme over coffee in the canteen.

And then of course, there is the advertising.

This is not designed to inform you about a product. This is designed to worry you and make you discontented, so you are only going to be happy again if you buy their product. (This incidentally, is not a theory; it is a proven method of advertising.) They tell you your house is crawling with germs and bacteria, and the only way to get rid of them is a large bottle of 'Splurge'. Or if your children don't take a certain type of yogurt they are going to be stunted unhealthy runts. It is all a load of bollox.

So advertising breeds discontent.

And the only way to satisfy this discontent is to try to make your house into a film set, or drive the latest SUV or buy whatever product is going to save you from a certain and nasty death. So you spend large amounts of money buying these things you don't need. And you get into debt. And the advertisers come along and say 'What? Will no one lend you money? We will lend you shed-loads more. Just phone 555-555-555', so you get even further in debt.

So television is turning the world into a society of debt-ridden, scared, discontented and unimaginative people.

I'd rant on a bit more, but my favourite programme is about to start.

EU LEGALISES HYPOCRISY

It is hard to practise what you preach.

For years now the EU has been telling us what is good for us. They told us that carrots had to be straight and eggs had to be a certain size. Then they started getting bolder and began messing with our laws.

That's fair enough. If a country has bad laws and is out of line with the rest of Europe, than it should be asked to change.

Now they are entering into the anti-smoking thing. They want to introduce a continent-wide ban. So far, Ireland, Scotland, Italy, Malta, Belgium and Sweden have signed up. England has also just joined the happy gang. Even France, that great bastion of smokers, has thrown in the towel.

So the EU decided that they should lead the way and introduce a smoking ban in their buildings in Brussels and Strasbourg from the 1 January 2007. They should set an example. They should show how easy it is. The rest of the EU will look to them as a shining beacon of health.

The ban lasted 43 days. They couldn't take it. They revolted in their masses.

'It is right for the Plebs and The Great Unwashed, but it is not right for us,' they cried.

'It is grand in theory, but we cannot take it,' they screamed.

In protest, they all lit up. Even non-smokers were lighting up. Several were reported to have died from asphyxiation and dozens more became addicted for life. The plume of smoke could be seen for miles.

They repealed the ruling. The EU buildings are once more a smoker's haven.

'The rule was not achievable,' a spokeswoman for Hans-Gert Poettering, the parliament's president, was quoted as saying.

The rest of us must do as they say, not as they do.

NEW DOGS ARE LEARNING OLD TRICKS

I felt like annoying someone this morning. It's not that I'm in a bad mood or anything. Just the opposite. I feel good.

However, I feel I am paying quite a lot for some services, so I feel justified in phoning them every now and again for my own amusement, and to annoy them. I have a bit of spare time and I have free phone calls, so why not?

I rang my broadband company. I went through the usual voice processing units and eventually got through to a nice girl. Well, she sounded nice anyway. So I explained my situation. I told her that they had upgraded their system last October but that they had only fixed mine last week. I explained that for the last five months I was paying for a better service, but was still receiving the lower grade, which was cheaper.

'Oh! I definitely think you are due a rebate,' says she and put me through to their accounts department.

I had to hold for about twenty minutes. Their music was bloody awful and a pain in the ear, but it gave me a chance to brush up on my Minesweeper skills (Expert Level, of course). I failed to beat my all time record but did manage to score 144, which isn't too bad.

A bloke eventually came on the line. He was foreign, of course, but at least I could understand him. In the beginning anyway.

I told him my story, and he said he would have to talk to his supervisor. He put me on hold. I went onto Solitaire this time. Boring, but it distracted me from the music.

He came back. I then realised I was beaten. He was worse than myself. He tied the conversation into knots, which is supposed to be *my* trick. I tried confusing him, but it was no good. He was a master at the art. I'm sorry now I didn't record the conversation, because I could have learned from this kid. I knew I was totally lost when he started talking about Tescos and the way they do promotional items. This lad was a genius! I had to concede defeat.

To console myself, I rang my waste disposal company. But the girl there was too nice. She laughed a lot and was very chatty, so I hadn't the heart to be a bastard. I just paid my yearly bill and quit.

Now I am depressed. I suppose it serves me right. I am depressed because sales people are beginning to learn my tricks. I am going to have to learn new ones.

There is a friend of Ron's that I phone from time to time. He has a habit of talking to his computer while he is talking to me, so in the middle of a conversation he will suddenly shout: 'Oh! You fucking idiot. Why are you doing that?' and I realise he is talking to the computer and not me. It is very confusing. But it's great. I must practise it.

Now, what's the number of the local Social Welfare Office?

THE DAY OF THE ECLIPSE

Herself dragged me into the local town yesterday. We don't go there that often, because it is noisy and the parking is difficult.

Normally you would find the usual mix of people walking the streets, but yesterday was different. It took me about a minute to realise this. I also noticed that there were massive traffic jams trying to get out of the town. I had wondered why I found parking so easily and why the traffic going into the town was so light.

The entire town seemed to be populated with a sort of sub-culture. The males all looked as if they had just popped out of the bookies after a twenty-year stint of staring at the screens. If they were American, they all would have been called Cletus. They had a Neanderthal, in-bred look about them – slack jaws, bulging eyes, knuckles dragging along the ground.

There were quite a few younger specimens too. There were all Gurriers and Snot Gobblers. They all had the mandatory mobile in one hand and a can of drink in the other. They communicated by whistles and by shouting at each other in an accent so thick even I couldn't understand it.

The females were the worst. They all seemed to be in their teens and all had the mandatory mobile in one hand and a pram in the other. And they all chewed gum with their mouths open. They were all dressed to look like Britney Spears. It seems to be compulsory to have at least one child by the time they are entering their teens. My theory is that, on entering puberty, they practise at home with the family. Either that or we have the highest rate of virgin births in the world.

The women were all eyeing up the talent. There was one who eyed me up. She was built like Mary Harney, but was wearing a mini-skirt and a top that was very low cut. The sight of that cleavage was as sexy as a plane crash, but just as fascinating. It was like two shaved pigs fighting in a hammock. I broke out into a cold sweat, but she passed by. Thank God.

I thought we might have wandered onto a film set, but there were no cameras around. It was strange. It was surreal. It wasn't threatening, but I felt uncomfortable. Herself didn't notice, but she had been into a couple of shops and was more interested in her purchases. I had stayed outside the shops and this was how I had had a chance to observe what was going on.

We got out of that town as fast as we could, which wasn't very fast as all the exit routes were still jammed with traffic.

Then it dawned on me. I wonder if the impending full lunar eclipse had anything to do with it?

YOU LOOK DOWN ON ME, THEN I'LL LOOK DOWN ON YOU

I hate snobbery. I also hate hypocrisy, but snobbery is up there with it.

I was enjoying my freedom the other night and went for a pint (or five). I met a bloke there as we stood outside in the rain having a smoke. It turned out he was from a village some distance from here.

'Yiz don't know how lucky yiz are livin' here,' says he. 'Our place is full of feckin' snobs.'

Apparently they built an estate outside his village and called it something like 'The Manor'. The houses were worth about €200,000 at the time, but the builder put them on the market for €800,000. The poor snobs fell for it. They snapped up the houses because they reckoned the riff-raff would be kept out by the prices.

They now think they own the village and look down on all the locals. And they all drive SUVs and park wherever they feel like it. They are worthless to the village because they all shop 'in Town' and socialise in the golf club.

To me, all people are equal in status. I might look up to someone I admire, like Stephen Hawking, but that's it. The only people I look down on are those who think they are superior to me by right of birth or wealth. And of course Skangers. But then everyone looks down on them.

My new pal told me about a time he drove down to the village and parked. He was getting out of his car when a big SUV pulled up beside him.

'I was going to park there,' said the SUV driver.

'I parked here first.'

'But that is my place. I always park there.'

'Wha?'

'That is my parking spot. I'm from The Manor, you know.'

I laughed. 'What did you say to that?' says I.

'I told him I was very sorry for his troubles,' says my friend. 'And then I told him to fuck off.'

LAMENT FOR A DYING BREED

Ron, Dick and I all live in the country. We like it here. It is nice and peaceful. You can see the stars at night, and listen to the owls hooting. During the day, we keep tally on the badgers, foxes and squirrels. The air is fresh and quiet.

We all live in roughly the same area, which is all back roads and lanes. When I first moved here over forty years ago, it was an event when a car went past.

Unfortunately, it is within commuting distance of Dublin. But everywhere in Ireland now seems to be within commuting distance of Dublin. So this means that the area is very popular for people to live in.

Now people have to live somewhere, and they are as welcome here as anywhere else. But I have a major complaint. This is the countryside. If you want to live here, then please respect that. Stop trying to turn it into suburbia.

Dick lives in a lovely old cottage. It's around 200 years old. A couple bought the house next door to him (another old cottage) and they are trying to turn it into something that wouldn't be out of place in the Docklands. They want to build a two-storey extension with a high blank wall along his boundary that would plunge his garden into darkness from midday on. He is livid. Apparently the couple want about five bedrooms, all en suite, with games rooms and saunas and God knows what else. If they want that, then why buy in the country? There are plenty of houses like that in suburbia.

Ron had wide open fields around his house. They are starting to build housing estates on them. He is depressed.

Where the cattle grazed, there will now be radios blaring in the summer and burglar alarms blaring for the rest of the year.

I'm not too bad at the moment, but they are threatening to build a housing estate the other side of the road. And we now have streetlights and footpaths. And I haven't seen a fox or a badger in a long time.

I'm not against progress. But let the people who want suburbia live in the suburbs, and let the people who want to live in the country respect it for what it is. Countryside.

If you want to build here, build something that is in keeping with the area. If you want a housing estate, then live nearer the city. If you want a five-bedroom house then build it where there are other five-bedroom houses. You will feel more at home there. After all, the people who live in the city sometimes want to go for a drive in the country. At this rate they are going to end up in Connemara before they find it.

So we are a dying breed, Ron, Dick and I. Along with the badgers, the foxes, the deer, the corncrakes, the bats, the squirrels, the field mice and everything else that likes a bit of space.

THE OLD TRICKS ARE THE BEST

Ron and I went for a few pints the other night. Ron and I have been pals for years. I am the quiet one. He is the one most likely to cause trouble. He is the kind of bloke who will get a full pint of water in a pub, put a beer mat over it, turn it upside down, put it on the counter and then whip the beer mat away. He does it for the hell of it. We've been thrown out a few times for that one.

Anyway, we were having a few. It was a friendly night, but the cash ran low.

'Fancy one for the road?' says Ron.

'No cash,' says I.

'Don't worry about that,' says he. 'There are always ways and means …'

He called the manager over.

'Excuse me,' says Ron 'but my friend and I are having a bet. He says there are four pints in a quart, and I say there are three. Could you set us straight?'

The manager laughed. 'Yiz are both wrong. There are two.'

He went away. Ron called the barman over.

'Same again,' says he, 'and it's on the house.'

'Yiz are joking,' says the barman. 'No one gets free pints here.'

'Well, the manager just said we could. Hold on. I'll clarify this,' says Ron.

'How many pints did you say?' he yelled at the manager.

'Two,' the manager yelled back.

'Funny,' says Ron to me, 'but they always fall for it. Even after all these years. Cheers,' says he as two fresh pints are placed in front of us.

2 APRIL 2207

Greetings, Grandad.

I was browsing the Tim Berners-Lee museum archives and I came across the original *Head Rambles* site from the early twenty-first century. We have the technology now to insert items into historical sites, so I hope you get to read this.

First of all, we (all your descendants) owe you an enormous debt of gratitude. You foresaw exactly where the sea level would rise to, and as a result of your foresight, we now own most of the north of the island of Leinster. This is one of the largest islands in the Irish archipelago, so we are quite well off.

I am living in a lovely seaside chalet on the beach at Tibradden not far from the port of Grandad that you founded near Ticknock. You would love it here. We are surrounded by coconut palm groves and the view is magnificent across the Dublin Sea to the Down peninsula in the north and the Isle of Snowdon to the east. The house is partly built into the mountain to help shelter us from the hurricanes and to keep us cool at midday. You would find the 40-degree heat a bit much.

I'm attaching a view from the house. You can just see the Down peninsula in the distance. No one quite knows what that stick thing is to the left. Archaeologists say it is part of the old Dublin, but I can't think what it was supposed to be for.

I suppose you would like to know what happened in the future?

As you know, George W. went against all advice and launched an attack on Iran. Of course they nuked the US and the North Koreans joined in for the fun. Bush and his cronies were lynched by a hysterical mob and the Radical Militia tried to take over. The Islamic Fundamentalists saw their chance and stepped in. We don't hear much from the Islamic Republic of America these days.

Of course, they were right about global warming and you will be pleased to note that you were right that it *is* a natural phenomenon. But before the people realised that, we had the mass riots in the middle of the twenty-first century. All SUV drivers were lynched and their vehicles burned. All air travel was banned and all aircraft destroyed. It didn't matter much anyway as at that stage most of the international airports were under water anyway.

There was a strange twist in history at the end of the twenty-first century. We had a visit from the Xyzzy spacecraft. They dropped off on their inter-galactic journey to a party in Alpha Centauri to say hello to the world. Apparently they have dropped in a few times in the past and were somewhat surprised that we were revering them as gods and prophets. Of course, this put paid to religion, but there are still a few die-hards. The Pope still lives in the Italian Alps with her husband and four children, but no one pays them much attention now. Of course, with the decline in religion, there was a corresponding decline in wars, so the world is quite a peaceful place now.

Your idea of abolishing elections was finally taken up and worked extremely well. Everyone was happy because they all had a say in things. Unfortunately, that more or less ended with the demise of the Internet, when all the networks got flooded. However, we have the NeuralWeb now where we communicate directly via thought transference. I don't know how you coped with all those keyboards and screens and things I've seen in the museum.

Television died the death around the middle of the twenty-first century. It had gotten to the stage where programmes were being stopped every five minutes so people could phone in to vote on what happened next. When this spread to the news channels, and people were voting on how many casualties they would like to see after an accident, the world decided to call a halt and all channels were taken off the air. The world is a better place for it.

The weather has changed a bit since your day. The winters are the most spectacular with the tornadoes and hurricanes hitting on a regular basis. The summers are nice. We just laze around supping our Vino Kippure produced from our own vineyards.

Life is good. Life is very very good.

Your great-great-great-great-great-grandson,

Grandad VII.

A HUMP OR A HOLE?

The county council are driving me mad. For some reason, best known to themselves, they've gone crazy digging the place up. They are digging holes in the road. They are digging trenches in the road. They are digging slots in the road.

The holes are round, square, oblong and rectangular. They are in no particular pattern. They are scattered at random along a half-mile stretch outside my house.

Now each time they dig a hole, they look into it and then fill it up again. And they finish it off perfectly, before moving on to the next one. And they're not moving gradually down, or up the road. When they finish one, they might move 3 yards or 300 yards before starting again. There is no pattern at all to it.

The thing that is bugging me (apart from the noise and the fact that I can't get out of my lane half the time) is the reason for it. I have been trying to work it out. I have come up with the following possible reasons:

They are looking for something. Maybe the last time they resurfaced the road, someone dropped something precious like a wedding ring or a mobile phone or a sandwich? And now they are digging in all the spots where he remembers standing? That can't be it, because they are going down very deep, and the bloke must have done a lot of standing around (there again?).

It's a Government Plot. They are looking for my Interweb connection so that they can silence me? If so, they'll have a job because all the wiring here is overhead and I use wireless anyway.

It's a Government Plot. Prior to the upcoming election, they are culling schoolchildren, the unemployed, the sick and homeless people, so that they can produce nice statistics. And they are burying the body parts under my road? Could be?

They are mining. They are finally laying the land mines I

requested, to keep the tourists away. I requested this a long time ago, as I'm sick of giving lost tourists directions up onto the bogs. This is a definite possibility.

It's a FÁS training thing. This has definite possibilities. It's all part of a training scheme. They are sending the trainees out to my stretch of road to practise their hole-digging skills. They are also being taught how to set up temporary traffic lights to cause maximum disruption.

At the moment, they are filling in the holes and doing a perfect job. You'd hardly know they'd been there. So the next lesson is how to finish the job with a hump or a hole.

Yes. That one looks like a runner.

NEIGHBOURS

There are a few houses up my lane. We are a quiet bunch, apart from the young family who hold craic parties from time to time and scare the shit out of Sandy with their fireworks.

Apart from throwing rubbish over each other's hedges we keep pretty much to ourselves. I don't see that much of them, as I seem to be the only one who wanders around the lane. I like to bring the sawn-off in case I meet a tourist. We get a few of them wandering around as, for some strange reason, they seem to think the lane goes somewhere. If they are young, female and pretty, I give them a quick grope and invite them to see my etchings. That gets rid of them sharpish. Anyone else, I shove the sawn-off up their backside and politely show them the road.

Yesterday, I was wandering around and met Brian. He was sitting on a sofa in the middle of the lane enjoying the sun. It seemed to be a strange place for a sofa, but it's none of my business. He invited me to join him.

I don't meet Brian much because he is one of the few residents who actually go out to work, so he's out most of the time. He's a nice bloke. We chatted for a while and then he said the dreaded words:

'I like your blog. Great laugh. I read it all the time.'

(Oh shit!)

'I've been telling all my friends about it.'

(Oh bollox!)

'Did you like what I wrote about yourself?' says I, being canny.

'Did you write about me?' says he, 'I didn't see any reference.'

(Major sigh of relief.)

I excused myself and rushed home. I had to spend all last night reading through everything I have written. Not a pleasant task. It's like going through the rubbish bin looking for a lost receipt. I think I'm in the clear. But I'll have to watch what I write in future!

EASTER TRADITIONS

I took a stroll down to the pub yesterday. Herself is not too well, and she wanted a sleep and I was fired out of the house.

Down in the pub we got talking about Easter traditions. The main consensus was that there weren't any. Most people just get tanked up on Saturday to make up for the Good Friday drought, and then spend Easter moaning about hangovers and eating chocolate.

So we decided it was time to start a new tradition. But what?

Some places have a tradition of rolling eggs down a hill, and this seemed like a good idea. But we had eaten all ours and there weren't any left. So we had to think of something else. Then someone spotted The Prat half dozing in a corner of the lounge.

The Prat fancies himself, and has declared he is going to run in the next election. He reckons he is going to be the new Taoiseach. In fairness, he couldn't be worse that the existing one, but he still isn't called The Prat for nothing.

We went over to him and nudged him awake.

'We would all like you to represent us. We are all agreed.'

His face lit up. He almost sobered up in his excitement.

'Jayzus lads. That's great. I'll sort out the crime and the potholes in the road and everything. I'll do anything for yiz.'

So we brought him out to the Sloping Meadow at the back of the village and pushed him off. He rolled very well. He was still floppy after the drink so he rolled in a fairly straight line. That was unfortunate, because he went straight through the clump of nettles and thistles half way down. He yelled a bit, but it was all part of the fun.

Unfortunately we forgot about the slurry tank at the bottom of the hill. The Prat scored a direct hit and went straight in. We stood around for a bit, but none of us was willing to go in there. We discussed it for a while and decided that this was a good tradition, and that we'd do it with any would-be politician who turned up in the area. And what's more, we wouldn't fence off the slurry pit, as it added to the sport. We decided to call it 'Prat Rolling' in memory of its first ~~victim~~ contestant.

We all went off home then, happy in the knowledge that we were at the birth of a new tradition that would probably last for hundreds of years.

MY DAD

I haven't written about my father before. He is a difficult man to write about. He died thirty-two years ago and I still miss him.

He was a very quiet man – quite the quietest I have ever met. But when he spoke, he was always worth listening to. He had a very sharp mind and a very dry sense of humour. He was a civil engineer by profession, but he should have been a philosopher. I remember one incident that gives a little insight.

Many years ago, we used to get a lot of Jehovah's Witnesses coming to our door. My mother used to slam the door in their face. But one day, she was out when they called. My father invited them in. I don't remember the exact conversation, but I remember the scene and the gist of it.

The two lads sat there in their immaculate suits, on the edge of the seat. Their faces were aglow. This was probably the first invite they'd had in weeks. They had all their pamphlets and were raring to go.

'What can I do for you?' says my Dad, lighting a cigarette.

'We have come to share the glory of our message,' they beamed. They looked like a pair of crows on a telephone wire.

'I don't believe in all that glory stuff,' said my Dad, without blinking. In fact he was a regular mass-goer, but he wasn't going to let that spoil a good debate.

So they spent half an hour trying to convince him of their message. They quoted the Bible at him. He quoted the Bible back at them. Every argument they would put up, he would counter it. I felt sorry for them. They hadn't a chance. I knew he could logically argue that black was white.

You have to understand that my Dad had nothing against these two. He wasn't trying to convert them. He just occasionally felt like a debate.

They began to get frustrated. They lost every argument, and eventually fell back on the basic argument that you must have faith.

'You must believe in God,' they said in desperation.

'Why?' said Dad. 'Why should I believe in anything when I don't know that anything exists?'

They were beginning to despair. I knew my Dad's argument on nihilism and it was his ace card.

'But you exist,' they said.

'How do you know?' said Dad. 'You imagine you see me, but I could be a figment of your imagination.'

'But we can see you and hear you, and you are talking to us,' they said.

'That could be all in your mind. You can't prove that I exist.'

They were sweating at this stage. They looked distinctly uncomfortable. Their pamphlets were in disarray. My Dad looked relaxed with his cigarette. He looked serious. He actually looked like someone who wanted to be convinced.

'But I know I exist,' said one, 'and I can see you and I can hear you so you must exist.'

'I know I exist,' said Dad, 'and I know I imagine I'm sitting here talking to two nice young men. You could come over and kick me in the shins, but I would just say that I imagined that you came over and kicked me. That doesn't prove anything. I know I exist, otherwise I couldn't have these thoughts, but the rest of it – you, the house, my son there – all of it could just be part of my imagination. You are all in my mind.'

They ran before he could change his mind.

SARTORIAL ELEGANCE

I wear clothes for three reasons.

I want to keep warm, as it can get quite chilly up in the mountains. I need somewhere to keep things like my tobacco and spare change and things like that. Lastly, I don't want to scare the children or make other men jealous. To me, clothes are a functional item. They arc there to serve a purpose and they do it well. So what do I like to wear?

Starting from the bottom, I like comfortable shoes. I have

a pair of runners that are *very* comfortable, but Herself has hidden them because she says they look shabby. This annoys me because they are like gloves – very light and comfortable – and they do the job of keeping sharp stones from between my toes.

Socks are fine, as long as they come above the ankles. I'm not worried about colour or whether they match or anything like that. Just so long as they stop my shoes chaffing my ankles.

Trousers I'm a bit more fussy about: 34-inch waist, 34-inch leg, zip up the front and pockets. Pockets are essential. They must be deep enough so that when I sit down, all my loose change doesn't fall out. I'm not worried about colour, so long as it isn't pink, white or green. Also I think polka dots look a bit clownish.

Shirts are easier. Any colour as long as I don't force people to wear sunglasses. But my shirt must have a breast pocket. That's where I keep my euro notes and my mobile. If I don't have a breast pocket, I'm lost. And I won't wear a shirt that has writing on it. Unless it's funny or obscene. I don't see why I should give anyone free advertising, or pretend to have been to an American university I've never heard of.

We were heading out for a drive yesterday, so I had another look for my runners (no go – she's damn good at hiding things) and put on a pair of shoes instead.

'You can't wear those shoes!' she shrieked.

'Why not?'

'You can't wear black shoes with brown trousers!'

I'm not privy to the black arts of Trinny and Suzannah, so I just changed my shoes. It's easier than arguing.

The fact that the black shoes are safer for driving in is irrelevant. The fact that they are more comfortable is of no consequence.

Herself is threatening to let the *Off the Rails* crowd on me to teach me the black art. I'd welcome that as it would give me a chance to bitch-slap (I believe that's the expression) that presenter with the Dublin 4 accent. I hate her voice.

I just don't understand this clothing thing. I like to wear clothes that are functional and comfortable (and have the right number of pockets). Herself likes me to wear things that are uncomfortable and non-functional, but look well. To me, comfort is the most important thing. To her, looks are the most important thing. I have a wardrobe of lovely comfortable jeans and trousers and shirts. I have a nice selection of shoes, boots and runners. But I can't wear any of them because they don't look good.

On second thoughts, I'll invite the *Off the Rails* team around myself. Apart from bitch-slapping Yer Wan, I might learn what the hell all the fuss about.

But I can't find my mobile. Herself insisted I wear the shirt I'm wearing. And it doesn't have a breast pocket.

THE DEVIL WEARS PRADA BUT DOESN'T SPEAK ENGLISH

Herself wanted to watch a film last night.

We have the Sky Satellite setup. It's an old one and not connected to the phone lines. So if we want to watch a film we have to ring them up. They then press a button or something and we can watch the film. Simple? No!

I rang Sky.

'Can I help you?'

Four words and I knew immediately I was in trouble. Another foreigner.

'I would like to book *The Devil Wears Prada* for half nine on channel 713, please.'

'Select ze channel and press ze select button on your control. Zat will book ze film.'

'No,' says I patiently. 'We don't have the box connected. We have to book it through you.'

There was a pause.

'Select ze channel and press ze select button on your control. Zat will book ze film.'

I knew I had a real one here! This was going to take a long time. I opened my special box of call centre Prozac and took a few. I explained as slowly as I could, in words of one syllable that I didn't have a phone connection on the box and that they had to release the film for me and that I had done it that way dozens of times in the past.

'Ze computer is broken,' says he.

'I don't care about your computer. I just want to watch a film! Can you please unlock the film for me?'

'Select ze channel and press ze select button on your control. Zat will book ze film.'

I hung up.

A couple of hours later, I rang back. It was getting close to the screening time at this stage.

'Can I help you?'

I don't know how many people they have in their call centre, but I had managed to get the same bloke.

'Is your computer fixed?' I asked.

'Yes. Ze computer is vorking.'

'Good,' says I. 'I would like to book *The Devil Wears Prada* for half nine on channel 713, please.'

'Select ze channel and press ze select button on your control. Zat will book ze film.'

'Listen dickhead,' says I (I knew I could swear at him – if he didn't have basic English he wouldn't understand and I would feel better), 'I explained all this before. All you have to do is take my name, address, codeword and you can release the film.'

'May I have your name pliz?'

I sighed with relief. We were getting somewhere. I gave him my name. It was a name he hadn't come across before, so we had great difficulty getting it across, but we got there in the end.

'May I have your address pliz?'

I knew I was in trouble. I don't live in an address like '5 The Green, Newtown'. I live in rural Ireland where we use townland names, which are derived from the old Irish names. I have a simple enough address – five words in total if you include the word county. It took fifteen minutes. I had to spell out each word, but he kept confusing 'm' with 'n' and 'b' with 'c' and the like. I even tried the phonetic alphabet – C for Charlie, but he didn't know what Charlie was and I even started to spell *that* for him. I was cracking up, despite the twenty Prozac I had taken at this stage.

Finally, I got my address through to him.

'May I have ze house number pliz?'

'I don't have a house number. I live in the country. We use house names. I have already explained that. I have given you my house name. Jayzus!'

He got the last word, and must have realised he was pushing it a bit so he skipped the house number bit.

'May I have your PIN code pliz?'

'WHAT?' says I. 'I don't know my PIN code. I have never been asked for my PIN code. You don't need my PIN code. And I would like to watch this film tonight, if at all possible!'

'Security,' says he 'Ve need your PIN for security.'

'I DON'T KNOW IT,' I shouted (five more Prozac). 'ALL I KNOW IS THAT IT STARTS WITH ZERO.'

He read the number out to me. 'Is zat it?' says he.

It suddenly dawned on me. A moment of complete frustration set in. I had to confirm my worst fears.

'Did you have all my information on the screen all the time?' says I.

'Yes. But I have to confirm for ze security.'

'Put me on to your fucking supervisor,' says I. Thirty Prozac wasn't enough at this stage.

'Ze film is booked,' says he. 'I am sorry if I hurt you.'

'Not half as sorry as I am that I can't hurt you,' says I and hung up.

Ten minutes later, we switched on to watch the film. A banner came up on the bottom of the screen: 'Press select for booking information'.

Ten more Prozac, and I reached for the phone. A very nice Scottish lass answered. I explained (in a hurry, as the film was about to start) what had happened and about the computer failure and all.

'There was nothing wrong with the computers,' says she. 'Can I have your details please?'

I gave her my name, address and password. It took all of ten seconds.

'Ah yes,' says she 'I see who it was. He's a bit of a dickhead.'

'Strange,' says I, 'that's what I called him.'

'Everyone does,' she laughed. 'He's managed to debit your account but he hasn't booked you any films.'

There was a fierce clattering of computer keys.

'You are OK now. I have cancelled the old booking and made a new one. And I'm very sorry about all that.'

I thanked her and sat back to enjoy the film, which had just started. *The Devil Wears Prada* is a good film. I normally don't like Meryl Streep as an actress but she was brilliant in this film. I just wish her character in the film could be dickhead's boss.

MOBILE PHONES

> If repeated often enough, a lie will become the new truth.
> *Paul Joseph Goebbels, Minister of Propaganda, Nazi Germany*

What exactly are the dangers of passive smoking? I have been trying to do some research on the Interweb, and I am finding some very conflicting evidence.

One research found that passive smoking is equivalent to smoking six cigarettes a year. Another quotes the following from a study of German flight crew:

> We found a rather remarkably low SMR (*standardized mortality ratio*) for lung cancer among female cabin attendants and no increase for male cabin attendants, indicating that smoking and exposure to passive smoking may not play an important role in mortality in this group. Smoking during airplane flights was permitted in Germany until the mid-1990s, and smoking is still not banned on all charter flights. The risk of cardiovascular disease mortality for male and female air crew was surprisingly low (reaching statistical significance among women).

So what is the risk? The entire basis for the smoking ban was to 'protect non-smokers in a smoking environment'. The key word here is 'protect' (i.e. to remove a potential harm). Most of the studies I found that proved passive smoking to be a danger were either biased or anecdotal.

So let's just say the jury is out on this one.

The jury is also out on the effects of mobile phones and phone masts. Yet I have seen no laws banning the use of mobile phones? Why? To me, the danger of mobile phone usage is possibly more important than the dangers of passive smoking.

I find mobile phones to be very irritating. I resent my peace being shattered by some bimbo shrieking that she is 'sooo not happy' at not being invited to someone's party, or some yuppy conducting some bit of ego-boosting business on the train.

I constantly have to be on the lookout for people who are driving while waffling on the phone. And I'm talking about hands-free phones here, before you all start moaning. They are concentrating so much on the conversation that they are completely unaware of their surroundings. The same goes for people on pavements. They barge around, pushing people onto the street because they are so wrapped up in some little domestic or social crisis.

And what of the dangers of radiation from all these phones around me? Not to mention the masts? Is my brain being constantly fried every time I go into town? Is this the cause of my insanity? What about the kids who get mugged, beaten up or even murdered for their phones? What about the invasion of privacy with the proliferation of camera phones?

Mobile phones are a far greater danger to public health than passive smoking. I just thought I'd run the idea up the flagpole and see who salutes.

IRELAND OF THE WELCOMES

Everything seems to be starting earlier in the year. The birds are nesting earlier. Insects are appearing earlier. Frogs are spawning earlier. And of course, tourists are arriving earlier.

Our first tourist was spotted in early February. I wrote to the *Irish Times* about it to see if it was a record, but of course they didn't print it.

This has led to some problems, as normally the Tourist Hunting Season doesn't start until 1 May. But some of us have been getting edgy, so we have jumped the gun, so to speak.

We are basically a rural community, and as such have great regard for wildlife. We have no truck with those bastards who go hunting for deer, badgers or foxes. These are dumb animals who can't speak for themselves, and hunting them is downright cruel. So we hunt tourists instead.

Tourists are arriving in ever increasing numbers. The government has done its best by inflating the price of everything to try to keep them out, but they are a major problem. They are filling up our roads, our hotels, our scenic spots and our pubs. They are loud and they are invasive.

Culling is the only answer. I know some of you will say it's cruel, but it is for their own good. And we are as humane as possible. We don't club them over the head or anything like that. We go for a good clean shot or a quick road kill. The numbers must be kept down, otherwise they will overrun the place and the indigenous species (the Irish) will be in endangered.

It is a very tricky sport, as tourists have an uncanny ability to disguise themselves as a native species. They have even stooped so low as to hire cars locally so that we can't tell them by the registration plates. Fortunately the car hire companies have co-operated by putting identification stickers on their vehicles. In the end, they always give themselves away. One will produce a camera, or another will wear shorts in the heat of the moment. We know the signs.

Even though the season has only just started, I am racking up quite a good score.

SEÁN

Seán is my grandson. He is a wonderful kid. He is inspirational.

Seán has cerebral palsy. When I tell people that, they say they are sorry. An elderly friend always refers to him as 'poor Seán'. There is nothing to be sorry about. Far from it. I'm not saying I'm glad he is the way he is – I'm not. Of course it would be great if he could run around and chatter away. But then he would be ordinary. And he wouldn't have given us that something special.

It is exceptionally unlikely that Seán will ever walk or talk. He will never run a race. So what? He will never write a book. The libraries are full of books. He will never drive a car. The road has enough cars. He will never give a lecture. Do we need another lecture?

Most people can do these things. But how many people can inspire pure love? How many people can make you happy just by their presence? How many people can, without saying a word, make you feel that the world is a better place?

People may say that Seán is a 'special person'. Seán is Seán. The only way he is special is that he has turned everyone who knows him into special people. We care for him. But we care for each other more too. He has made us softer and more gentle. He has brought out the caring in us. He has made us more tolerant.

In my own case, I do what I can for the Jack and Jill Foundation. They looked after him and his mother so well when they needed help the most. Even though Seán is no longer on their books (because they provide respite care for the parents of young babies), I still want to help them (and they are always in need of a few bob). They do fantastic work and without Seán I probably would never have heard of them.

They helped our K8 when she was in crisis, when she was coming to terms with being the mother of a disabled child. Now she is just the mother of Seán. We don't see him as disabled. We see him as a lovely, loving child. Mind you, he's nearly six now, so he is a young boy.

Seán may not talk to us, but he talks to the angels. He sits quietly, smiling to himself. He will laugh with us. Seán will never ever laugh at us. But I think he can see a world that we can't see.

Seán – the world would be a much poorer place without you.

PUPPYCHILD

I wrote yesterday about Seán, but I do have a granddaughter too. She must be feeling a bit left out at this stage.

When she was newly born and brought out to the house here, we had to introduce her to Sandy.

So I explained to Sandy that she was a man-puppy. Sandy is very maternal and is very gentle with all living things (except cats, of course). If a bird flies into the window and falls to the ground, Sandy will gently nudge it until it flies off. So I had no real worries about her harming the baby.

Her name has changed over the years to Puppychild. She is two and a half now. She is a very bright child. She has a great sense of humour and we always end up in fits of laughter when she is around.

The other day, she was visiting. I was sitting watching her. She was standing looking very solemn, and gazing into the distance. I looked at her over the top of my glasses, because that's what grandads are supposed to do.

'What are you thinking?' says I.

She turned and looked at me. She stared at me for a moment. Her expression never changed. She then moved over to me and gently pushed my glasses back up to the top of my nose. She went back to gazing into the distance. I could hear her thoughts:

'Stupid Grandad. He doesn't know how to wear his glasses. I showed him.'

She also has a great sense of timing. Our K8 told the story of being stopped at a police checkpoint.

She and Puppychild were driving home from the shop when they were stopped. It was one of those checkpoints to see if your car tax and insurance are up-to-date and things like that. K8 wound down the window and the policeman stuck his head in the window.

'It's a pig!' shrieked Puppychild in delight.

Any child that would take one look at a policeman and say 'it's a pig' has to be OK in my book.

HANG A RIGHT AND CHILL OUT

There has been a focus recently on the standard of literacy amongst our young people. The main focus was on text-speak, as it's called.

I can understand people using text shorthand on mobile phones, where letter count is at a premium, but I abhor its use anywhere else. I just won't read it. If people cannot be bothered to take the trouble to write properly, then I can't be bothered to read their message.

They say that text-speak is lowering the standard of spelling. Slipelng is not as mcuh an issue as many plpoee thnik, as raseecrh sohws that txet may stlil be lgbeile no matter how iorneccrt the slieplng. Pvdiored the lteters are tehre, and the fsrit and lsat ltretes are crcerot, tehn the oedrr of the inrveneitng lrtetes is not that inpomtart. Msot peploe sluhod be albe to read tihs prgaparah!

I would argue that it is not the mobile phone that has led to a drop in standards, but rather a drop in the standard of education in our schools and the overuse of television.

Simple rules are not apparently taught any more. I have heard university students using the ubiquitous 'I done' and 'I seen' instead of 'I did' and 'I saw'. And no one seems to know the basic use of an apostrophe any more.

But what really annoys me the most is the use of words without any consideration for their meaning. For this, I have to blame television. People are using words simply because they are in vogue. They are destroying the language by peppering it with expressions they have heard on *Friends* or *Lost* or whatever programme is the flavour of the month.

For example, 'hot', 'cool' and 'chill' are words that refer to temperature. How can they possibly be used to mean 'good', 'good' (!) or 'relax'? What does 'check out' mean? How can that possibly be translated as 'take a look at'? When giving directions, what does 'take a right' mean? Or even worse, 'hang a right'. Why are people stealing a junction, or even worse, executing it? What's wrong with 'turn to the right'? And for the sake of my sanity, please stop saying 'you guys'! A guy is a rope for supporting a tent. In slang, it means a man. Now it apparently means everyone.

I love language. It has always been a bit of a hobby of mine. I never studied English beyond leaving certificate standard, so doubtless I sprinkle my writings with split infinitives and other grammatical errors. But I do my best. I know language has to evolve, but let the evolution be logical. I can understand how the word 'bouse' became 'booze', but I cannot understand how 'good' can become 'cool'.

One very interesting phenomenon that I have noticed is the very high standard of literacy amongst bloggers. It is in marked contrast to discussion forums where text-speak and general illiteracy seem to be common. That would be an interesting subject for a thesis!

And now, having got that lot off my chest, I'm going to chill out, leave you guys alone and go back to my own cool crap level of writing.

OLD-STYLE SHOPPING

When I was a lad, we lived about a mile and a half from Terenure. In those days, we had fields behind us where they kept the horses that used to pull the HB milk carts. Now there isn't a field for miles.

If we wanted groceries, Terenure was the nearest shopping area. We used to walk there, unless it was raining, when we'd get the bus. We had a car, but that was kept for important trips only.

Terenure was still a village then. The main grocery shop was Floods. It's long gone now. It had great oak counters, with lines of biscuit tins in front. The biscuit tins had transparent lids so you could see the contents. There was a lovely smell of smoked bacon and spices. You would be served by a cheerful assistant, who would fetch each item in turn off the shelves behind him. Items such as sugar and butter had to be weighed and packaged. Very few items were pre-packed in those days.

When the time came to pay, you gave the assistant the money. He would put it and the bill into a wooden jar that was then clipped into an overhead wire system. He would pull a handle and the wooden jar would go flying across on its wire into the cash office, which was high on the opposite wall. There, a girl would put in the change and the receipt, and the jar would come flying back again.

Choice of food was very small compared to nowadays. There were no exotic fruits or vegetables. There were only a few varieties of other products such as breakfast cereal or tinned produce. You could only buy fruit or vegetables if they were in season. But they tasted great! People nowadays have no idea how food really tastes. Unless of course, you grow your own. In those days bread was lovely and soft and squishy, with crackly crusts on the outside. Fruit and vegetables had real flavour.

Across from Floods was Home Stores. I loved that shop. It was a smallish hardware shop and was jammed to capacity with produce. You could buy anything there. They had gardening tools and carpenters tools. They sold wood and rope. If you wanted a single nail, you could buy one. Nails were usually sold by weight. Nothing was pre-packaged. I presume they are long gone too.

The chemist was another shop I remember well. Again, if you wanted a prescription, it had to be made up by the chemist. He would vanish into the back and return a while later with The Bottle. The Bottle was usually small, with a handwritten label and a cork in the top. If the contents were poisonous, it would be a special bottle with ridged sides, just to warn you.

Then there was Eaton's the bakery. Everything was fresh, from the doughnuts to the bread. And the smell in that shop was fantastic.

Nearly all of that is gone now. Terenure is more of a traffic jam on the way into the city now. I haven't been there in a while, and I am unlikely to pass through.

I miss the personal service of those old shops. I miss the ability to buy a single battery instead of four. I miss the days when you could open a pack of rashers without a degree in engineering, or a very sharp pair of scissors.

But most of all, I miss the taste of food.

HOLIDAYS

What is it about Irish holiday cottage rentals? Why do they always seem to assume that there are eight of me?

I have been idly trawling the Interweb looking for a place to rent for a week or so in west Cork. We might go. Then again we might not. But there is no harm in looking. The problem is that there are two of us. Just Herself and myself. But can I find a small place? Can I hell!

Every place I find proudly boasts 'sleeps six' or 'sleeps eight'. How often do you get eight people going on holiday together? I suppose there are families with six children, but not that many these days. Or are we supposed to drug our friends and bring them too and force them to pay their share? Because these places seem to charge by the bed.

Last year we stayed in France in a gîte that had four beds. Ideal. We used the upstairs room as a storeroom and slept in the main bedroom. The upstairs room was so small that you had to be a contortionist to get into it anyway. The two previous years we went Up North and stayed in a cottage that could (at a pinch) sleep four. Ideal.

But here, they seem intent on giving us top end luxury we don't want. Why on earth should we want a jacuzzi and en suites when we don't have them at home? Why do we have to have DVD players in every room? We're on holiday, for God's sake!

All we want is a small, comfortable basic house. Preferably with a roof. (We once booked a place that was advertised in the paper and it turned out to be a shed with no roof! Luckily we didn't pay a deposit.) We want a bedroom, preferably with comfortable beds, a basic kitchen, a bathroom and a sitting-room. We're not pushed about television, except maybe for the weather forecast (who wants to watch the news on holiday?). I can manage quite well without a swimming pool, or a sauna, or a barbecue, or a phone. I don't need a dishwasher or a washing machine. I don't need ironing facilities and I can bring my own hairdryer (which I don't use anyway). I don't need baby-sitting services, as I can trust Herself to look after herself when I'm down the pub. She's old enough now.

As for location, we want peace and quiet. No immediate neighbours. No play areas. A view would be nice. And it should be within staggering or even crawling distance of a pub.

It's not much to ask. Is it?

ROUTINE

When I was a child, everything had its time and its place. The days were marked by events.

Saturday was bath day, when we all bathed and washed our hair (not all together, I hasten to add). Because Sunday was mass day.

Sunday was a big deal. First of all no breakfast, because in those days, you had to fast from midnight. Then we'd head off to mass in the car. Sunday was about the only day in the week when we got a ride in the car. Mass, of course was the old style. We stared at the back of the priest as he chanted away in Latin and it all had a great air of mystery. None of this lets-all-be-friends-and-shake-hands stuff. The mass then had an air of timeless ritual.

On Sunday afternoon, if my Dad was in a good mood (which he usually was), we'd go for The Sunday Drive. This could be anywhere – Slane, the Wicklow mountains, Howth. I never knew where we'd end up, but it was fun.

Monday was wash day. My mother would fire up the big copper boiler, and all the sheets and cloths would be left to boil and the place would fill up with steam. And after they had boiled for while, we had to put them through the wringer and then hang them out on the line. None of your washing machines and tumble-driers for us!

The days themselves had little milestones too. Meals were *always* eaten at the table. It wouldn't occur to us to eat anywhere else. And we had to get permission to leave the table! On hot summer days, we used to lay the table in the garden and eat out there. Dinner was at one o'clock sharp. Tea was at five. If you were late, then too bad.

A quarter to two was *Listen with Mother* with Daphne Oxenford, on the radio. My day was incomplete without that (I was only three or four, for God's sake). At two, I had to be silent for an hour. This was *Woman's Hour* time, and my mother would stretch out on the settee with her cup of tea and a digestive biscuit. I used to get my dose of Virol then too. I loved Virol. It was like liquid toffee. I wonder what happened to it?

Evenings were spent around the fire. This was the time for reading or listening to the wireless. Sometimes my dad would put on a record. It was all very cosy.

Nowadays, people eat around their widescreen televisions that dominate the room. Meals are whenever you want them. Conversation is a dead art. Studies have shown that one of the causes of juvenile delinquency is the decline in the formal family meal. Children identify more with their friends and characters on television than they do with their families. Sad.

I must admit to eating in front of the television myself these days. We have a washing machine and a tumble-drier. The car is used whenever we feel like it.

I listen to the radio a lot. But the biggest thing I have brought with me from those days is my love of books. I'd be lost without my books.

AND THE WINNER IS ...

I have been hearing a lot lately about Opinion Poles. Everyone seems to think they are great.

If the party is looking good in the poles, then 'poles are the voice of the people'. If the party is looking bad then 'we don't pay much attention to the poles. It's the election that counts'.

In its eternal quest for truth, *Head Rambles* has decided to do its own pole.

So I headed off. The first pole I came across was a telegraph pole. It was plastered in election posters. Someone had shot Bertie Ahern through both eyes with a .22 (good shooting, by the way!). It gave him a rather blank and vacant look. Very realistic, I thought.

I headed on, passing many poles and they were all plastered with posters. On one of them, Michael McDowell was hanging upside down. He looks much better that way. You should try it permanently, Michael. Your ratings might go up.

Eventually I ended up in a shopping centre with one of those big department stores. This is where I found my Pole at last.

'Hello,' says I. 'Are you a Pole?'

'Cześć,' says he.

'OK. You are a Pole, and I want your opinion.'

'Nie rozumiem.'

'Who do you think is going to win the election?'

'Kocham Cię,' he replied.

This wasn't going as well as I'd hoped.

'Which coalition would you prefer to see in power?'

'Jestem w ciąży. Wyjdziesz za mnie?'

'Who would you like to see as Taoiseach?'

His face lit up. He ran off and came back with a tee-shirt with 'FCUK' written across the front.

'Which is the best party?' says I.

He ran off again, and came back with twenty Silk Cut.

'And which party will support them in government?'

Once again, he disappeared and came back with a bra (I think it was a 40DD). He thought he was getting the hang of this.

'And the opposition?' says I. 'Do you think the Greens will be in government or in opposition?'

He looked puzzled for a moment, but then did his vanishing trick again. He came back with a cabbage and a load of green beans. My carrier bag was getting fairly full at this stage so I thanked him.

'Nie mogę bez Ciebie żyć,' he replied.

So there you have it. The official *Head Ramble* Opinion Pole.

The result? We are going to have a FCUK as Taoiseach, with a party of fags in power. They will be supported by a bra. And the Opposition will be a load of vegetables.

WHAT IS THE POINT?

In the old days, the heart of Dublin was Nelson's Pillar. It was the focus of the city. It was marked as the destination on buses going to the city.

I used to love that pillar. For 6 pennies (a tanner) you could enter the dark doorway, and climb the spiral staircase inside, right to the top. The view was fantastic. The flower and fruit sellers used to have their stalls around the base. It was a meeting place. I loved it.

In 1966 the IRA blew it up. The bastards. It was supposed to represent 'British imperialism' or something. Crap. It was an icon of the city.

They should have left the stump as a monument to stupidity. Instead it was removed and replaced with a fountain. That was an ugly yoke. It was a figure of a very depressed looking female sitting in a tub. It was supposed to represent the River Liffey. It became known as 'The Floozie in the Jacuzzi' and became a handy place to dump your old beer cans and McDonalds junk. It was removed.

I can't describe what replaced it. It's not a monument. It's not a statue. It's certainly not a building, even though they employed a firm of architects to 'design' it. I don't know how much training they had to learn to draw a straight line? It cost nearly 5 *million* euro to put up. But what is it?

It is completely functionless. If they grew sweet pea plants up it in the summer, it would be nice. If they had drilled holes through it, it could have made a fluting noise in the wind. If they had attached mobile phone antennas at the top, it would have a purpose. Come to think of it, a mobile phone mast would have been more attractive. It is supposed to be self cleaning. I have this vision of it waiting until no one is looking and then shaking itself like a dog. And they still have to clean it every year!

It has, of course attracted a load of colloquial names: Bertie's prick; Stiletto in the Ghetto; Erection at the Intersection; Stiffy by the Liffey. I don't like it, because there is nothing to like. I don't dislike it, because there is nothing to dislike. I just wish someone would tell me what it is, or what it does, or what does it represent?

What is the point?

STOP THE WORLD - I WANT TO GET OFF

When I retired, I wondered what I was going to do with my time.

The old cliché is that I take up golf or oil painting or fishing. But I'm not very good at those. They didn't appeal. So I set up a little business.

I always wondered what it would be like to run a business; to make my own decisions, with no one telling me I'm late in the morning or that I'm not turning the treadwheel fast enough.

I knew nothing about business. I knew the simple basics like not selling something for less than what you paid for it. I knew that the customer is always right, even when they're wrong. But that was about it.

I thought it would be nice when someone asked me what I did for a living and I could reply that I 'owned my own business' (you have to imagine that last phrase with an 'evening cocktails' kind of voice). As it was more of a hobby than anything else, I decided never to advertise it.

'What kind of eejit starts a business and makes a decision not to advertise it?' I hear you ask. My kind of eejit. I'm weird in that kind of way. Anyway, I hate ads.

'What kind of business is it?' you ask.

'Mind your own business,' says I, because that would be advertising (but it's a kind of consultancy business. That'll do you for now).

I thought it would be a handy excuse if ever I was asked to do the washing up ('sorry, I have to do my accounts') or go shopping ('sorry, I'm expecting a phone call'). I didn't think anything would actually *happen*.

But the damn thing took off and has a life of its own. Even though people had never heard of me, they started contacting me. Strange. I got some very big clients. And they started spreading the word. And then I got even more clients.

Now this was fine. I was occupied. And money was coming in. I could afford to renew the car. We could go to France on our holidays. There was the downside of course – I had to do book-keeping, which I *hate*. I never realised there was so much involved, because I had always been an employee and someone else always looked after these things. But now I'm on my own.

Things were actually starting to get a bit hectic. I was actually back to doing a nine to five job. Except, when you run your own business, you don't knock off at the stroke of five, because there is always something important that has to be done. I was working harder in retirement than I had been when I was working. If you know what I mean.

So, last autumn, I decided to retire from my own business. I would keep my existing clients, in case they needed me, but that was it. No more new work. I could relax and read and do some gardening and play with blogs and the like.

It didn't work. The phone calls keep coming in. I still don't know where they come from so I started asking them (that's called market research – I'm learning!). It turned out all my existing clients are telling their pals and giving out my phone number.

The last few days have been hectic. I have two new big clients. One was a tender I had been asked to submit about a year ago. I had forgotten about it but they emailed me, and I'm to start work straight away. New clients are ringing on a fairly regular basis. I don't like to tell them I'm retired, because that might scare my existing clients if the word spread. I don't like to tell them to fuck off, because I'm really a very nice bloke. The only people I swear at on the phone are call centres and people doing surveys.

So I had an idea. I'd raise my prices, so they would go somewhere else, and my existing clients would think they had a bargain. But they keep accepting the quotes. So I still have more business coming in.

I'm feeling more like Reggie Perrin every day.

A FLOATING VOTER FINALLY SINKS

I was a floating voter up to yesterday. So I floated down to the polling station to see what would happen.

The place was deserted except for a very bored looking garda and a few people sitting behind boxes. They looked like they were expecting thousands to arrive, and all started fighting to get me over to their table because I was the only person there. And Herself of course.

Being a very conscientious person, I had recycled my polling card a couple of weeks ago, but that didn't bother them. I just told them that I was famous and that was good enough.

So I cast my vote and went looking for the exit poll that they are always talking about. I found the exit, but no Poles. There were a couple of Lithuanians beating the crap out of each other, so I shot them. There was also a very beautiful blue butterfly on the ground. I carried him to a bush in case someone stepped on him.

I suppose you want to know how I voted? I'm not in Bertie's or Harney's or McDowell's constituencies so there was nothing I could do about them. So I crossed the first candidate off the list and printed in Grandad. I gave myself number one, of course. Herself did the same. So if no one else turns up, I'm elected.

And the rest? Well, they are all pretty much the same when the dust settles. I still couldn't decide. Then it struck me. The perfect vote!

I gave them *all* my number twos.

A LITTLE RETROSPECTION

A few nice things happened yesterday.

Jimmy called round and we discussed some home improvements. Jimmy is the handiest handyman/fixer/builder that I know and he has some great mates who are top-rate electricians and plumbers. We are going to do a little refurbishing in the kitchen and Jimmy dismissed all my fears of a 'big job'. So that is a weight off my mind.

We also arranged for a bloke to come around and do some heavy gardening that has been worrying me for a while. Another weight gone.

And the PDs got crapped on. From a great height. Good riddance. It couldn't have happened to a nicer bunch of people.

Now that the dust is beginning to settle on yesterday, things don't look too bad. We are in for some 'interesting' times. Bertie may end up as Taoiseach, but he is either going to have to rely on a lot of independents and the Greens or he is going to have to sway Labour. I can't see the latter happening, but if it did, it's going to be a mad coalition. But it would be the end of Labour. I doubt anyone would ever trust them again. Whatever happens, I can't see us ending up with a stable government.

Another very strange thing happened last night. I saw Bertie being interviewed, and I actually liked him. Just for a moment. He came across as humorous and reasonably intelligent. He was coherent. He made sense. He was relaxed. He slagged off journalists (which didn't amuse John Bowman). He was *likeable*.

And then I remembered the state of the country and the moment passed.

So I'm back now to planning the revolution. It's the only thing that makes sense. I will make an excellent leader. I'm honest. I'm not corrupt. I will keep my word. I will put the people of this country first. But I need financing.

So if there are people out there who would like to send me some bulging brown envelopes? I have set up the offshore account and the biggest donors will get the best jobs.

Things are going to change.

ANYONE FOR TEE?

By now you probably know I hate sport. I have played a little tennis in my time. I played hockey once by accident, and they tried to make me play rugby at school.

The only sport I ever really took to was golf. Well, by golf, I mean par-3. Until a couple of years ago, I had never wielded anything bigger than a three-iron.

It's an old cliché that retired (or semi-retired) people take up golf. It never occurred to me to do anything like that. It costs a lot to join a club and you need all sorts of things like golf clubs. But I quite like playing. It is a relaxing sort of game. There is no hysteria, like in football. You can talk golf without having to know the name and score of every player back to the 1940s. It is played in pleasant open spaces where you can enjoy nature, and it is good exercise.

There is something immensely satisfying about a good tee shot. There is the crisp click as you hit the ball square on and then watch as it sails high over the trees to be followed by the sound of breaking glass and a yell from some unfortunate.

Our K8 was here over the weekend. She told me she had bought some clubs for The Accidental Terrorist for his birthday. He had immediately gone out and completed the set. But he already had a full set which is now redundant. So she informed me that his entire old set is now in my porch. It's mine.

All I need now is someone to play with and somewhere to play. None of my pals around here play, so it's a bit of a problem. I'm going to play around the garden a bit. I have enough space to play with putters and 9 irons and maybe even 7 irons. I'll have to cut the grass more often though. I can practice my drives by aiming for the neighbour's windows.

Our K8 is moving to a new house close by soon, and she says we are going to play a lot on the course up the road. That sounds great, but I think they've closed the course down, which is a bummer.

My ambition is to be the first person ever to get a hole in one on a par 5 at the US Masters at Augusta. Does anyone know where I can get an application form?

ELECTRICITY IS THE SPARK OF LIFE

The electricians called yesterday.

I had better explain (briefly). Herself is an avid fan of those programmes on television that show houses being done up and given makeovers (God, how I hate that word – it's meaningless and ubiquitous). She keeps saying that 'we must get something like that' or 'that would look lovely here'. So she started on about the kitchen. After several belts of the frying pan, I relented and said she could have her kitchen makeover. This involves a new ceiling and a new floor. And the new ceiling involves concealed lighting. Hence the electricians.

There were two of them – the Gaffer and his Jimmy. I asked if they wanted the power off and they looked insulted. They gave me that look as if to say 'we are professional electricians. We are used to working on live wires. Only pansies switch the power off.' So I left them to it.

The Jimmy shinned up onto the kitchen sink and began messing with the existing fluorescent tube. There was a very pretty blue flash and the Jimmy ended up on the flat of his back on the floor. The Gaffer and I stood looking at the Jimmy as he lay there.

'You'd better give him the kiss of life,' says he.

'No fucking way,' says I, 'I don't know where he's been and I've never kissed a man in my life.'

'It was your electricity.'

'He's your Jimmy.'

We argued the toss and, eventually, the Gaffer decided he'd better do something. But in the meantime, the Jimmy had vanished. He returned shortly to say that he had thrown the master switch and all the power was off.

'Are yiz all right?' says the Gaffer.

'Grand,' says the Jimmy, 'it woke me up nicely.'

So I left them to it and went back to my work. But the computer of course was dead. And all my work was gone. Bugger!

They've gone now, and the ceiling is a spider's web of cables hanging all over the place. There are a couple of naked bulbs hanging down, so I keep hitting my head off them. The place is a mess until the carpenters can come to fit the ceiling.

I'm going to have to get rid of that damned television.

GET RID OF THE REMOTE CONTROL

Welcome to our latest law in a long stream of idiotic laws.

It is now illegal to buy or sell packs of ten cigarettes.

Even those shops that still have packs of ten in stock can't sell them. So any child who used to buy a ten pack will now buy a twenty pack instead. Congratulations legislators, on your incredible bid to increase under-age smoking.

This law ranks up there with the law that bans the burning of wood in a garden, yet you can get a grant to install a wood burning stove in the house!

Fifty years ago, I was unaware of the law in the course of my daily life. I was aware that there were laws about theft and damage to property. And of course, murder was frowned upon. But as I was brought up not to kill, steal or vandalise, these laws didn't bother me.

There was the time I trespassed to collect conkers: the police just reminded me that it was private property and that I should ask permission first. That was the way it was. If you broke the law, you were given a rap on the knuckles. Unless of course it was a really serious offence. In our day-to-day lives, we cycled without helmets. We roller-skated without protective clothing. If we went boating, we never bothered with floatation jackets. We could buy a single cigarette. The only place I remember smoking being prohibited was downstairs on the bus. We saw the law as something serious, but it was for criminals. The rest of us respected one another and if we harmed ourselves, that was our problem.

Now there is legislation governing just about every aspect of our lives. And what's worse, the authorities are determined to catch us out. They install speed traps, closed-circuit cameras and smoke detectors. They deliberately set out to catch people breaking laws. The law is no longer there to protect – it is there to control.

As a result, the man in the street (like me) feels like he can't be trusted. He is being treated like a child and every move is being watched 'for his own good'. And it is in the nature of the child to rebel, and to push the boundaries.

I am a citizen of this state and as such I am entitled to my liberties. And those liberties include the right to make my own mistakes and to harm myself, provided of course I am not harming others.

Doubtless they will bring in legislation at some stage to outlaw unprotected sex or the use of DIY tools. Maybe a law prohibiting the wearing of shoes with the laces undone? Or the amount to food we can eat? Where does it stop?

The child in me is rebelling. I give two fingers to a lot of the laws because they are trying to control me, not protect me. I am old enough to know myself what is good and what is bad.

I know it will only get worse. The government wants to control the people and there is little I can do about it. I will continue to object.

Until blogs become illegal of course.

LET THERE BE LIGHT

I wrote earlier about the new ceiling. Since then I have been getting up at the crack of dawn each day to let the builders in, because they insist on starting at the crack of dawn and I have to let them in.

In case you wonder why it took so long to put up a

ceiling, I'd better explain that the roof is supported by old timber beams that look rather nice. So instead of covering up the beams, they put the ceiling in-between the beams. So in fact they had to put up twelve ceilings. One between each pair of beams.

They are finished now. They did a brilliant job. It was very hard work, and I learned a lot of new language and was reminded of some nice words and expressions I'd forgotten.

The electricians are back today to fit the lighting. They arrived this morning. They unscrewed all the light switches so that they are all dangling off the walls. And then they disappeared again. I think they may have gone off to Dublin to switch off the power station. Just in case. You can't be too careful with electricity.

So if half of Leinster is plunged into darkness, I'm sorry. But Herself wants a new ceiling and lighting so we all have to make sacrifices.

PLUG AND PLAY MY BACKSIDE

I have one of those wireless thingies for my computer. It had a hissy fit yesterday and I couldn't do anything with it, so I decided to reset it this morning. I pressed the little reset button on the back, and that is when the fun began.

You see I'd lost the manual for the wireless thingy and also all the settings that my broadband people had given me. So I rang them. I got through straight away, which was a miracle. But it was karma playing a joke on me, because I got onto a bloke who was so foreign I could only understand about one word in ten.

We held the conversation purely by guesswork. If I didn't understand anything he said, I would say something at random, like my address or phone number. The odd time, I would pick out a word and we'd make some progress. Eventually, after about ten minutes, I got the information I wanted. The whole thing wasn't helped by the fact that his records showed that I had been disconnected about a year ago and didn't exist any more. I sometimes think that myself.

So I started putting the numbers into my wireless thingy. I kept denying myself permission to get into it, like cutting off the branch you're sitting on. So I had to keep resetting it. The reset button is getting a bit worn now.

I got it working eventually and I am back into the Interweb. I've wasted a whole morning of ~~porn~~ research though.

If I buy a new toaster and bring it home, I just plug it into the wall and make my toast. Why can't computers be the same? They used to rant on about plug-n-play or whatever you call it, but it isn't like that. You'd need a Masters degree in advanced mathematics to get one of these yokes running.

And they wonder why there aren't many of us old folks on-line?

CHEFFY'S VOMIT

When I was ten, I was sent to boarding school. I soon discovered that this wasn't a place where merry chaps played cricket and then had a pleasant evening roasting a first-year pupil over an open fire. This was more like Colditz – a dark place where survival was the name of the game. For this was Ring College (or Coláiste na Rinne, as they liked to call themselves) where we could only speak Irish and you were punished if a word of English slipped out.

Mercifully, my memory auto erased itself to spare me the nightmares of the place, but one or two still linger.

One of my memories was of Cheffy's vomit. This was the main meal of the day on Friday. It was revolting stuff. It had the look and consistency of wallpaper paste and had little things like diced carrot floating in it. It was bland and had a taste of desperation about it. It was served up in a soup dish and we all ate it or starved. I'm sure we should have been entitled to Red Cross parcels, but we were too young and scared to argue.

But why do I think of Cheffy's vomit now?

Strangely, it was the news of the Greens' pact that brought the memories back. Our current selection of political parties are the Cheffy's vomit of the modern day. They are colourless, tasteless and we put up with them because that's what we are given. But there was always that little bowl of peas at one side of the soup dish. I don't fancy a diet of peas, but at least it was there, providing a bit of colour and an alternative if you were desperate.

Now the peas have been thrown into the vomit. It is the end of alternatives. It is the end of the mildly eccentric bit of colour. We are now stuck with Cheffy's vomit for the foreseeable future and it makes me want to throw up.

I know some will say that there are still different flavours in government. But it is very hard to tell the difference. Maybe a 1 per cent difference in proposed tax rates, or a difference of opinion as to where private hospitals are built, but essentially they are all the same recipe.

What we need now in Irish politics is a bit of spice. A vindaloo on the menu, or a bit of bolognese. Even a traditional Irish stew would do to liven things up a bit.

Anything but Cheffy's vomit.

THE ROAD LESS TRAVELLED

I like messing around with new technology. What bloke doesn't? So, when a pal of TAT's offered me a loan of one of those new in-car navigation systems, I had to take him up on it. They always intrigued me, not only with their vast knowledge of our road systems, but also the way they know where you are all the time.

We installed it yesterday and I thought I'd try it out. I wanted to hear it tell me how to get to the village, which is a mile down the road. So I programmed in my location and told it where I wanted to go. And off I went.

I normally turn right at the end of the lane and was a bit surprised when a sexy female voice told me to turn left. But with a voice like that, how could I refuse? Maybe it knew a shortcut I had never heard of?

It was very seductive, being given these silky instructions on where and when to turn, and I trusted it completely. I began to have some doubts when I found myself paying the motorway toll at Drogheda, but I was sure the nice girl knew best. So I carried on.

It's a long time since I had been to Sligo, and Benbulbin looked nice through the rain. Another place I can recommend is the lakes of Killarney at sunset. They looked beautiful and mysterious.

I began to have my doubts about sexy girl's instructions somewhere outside Bristol. This did seem rather a long shortcut. So I asked her if she was lost. She remained confident, but I was getting worried. So I reprogrammed her to take me home again.

I'm not quite sure why she chose a route through Amsterdam, but I had never been there before, and it is a beautiful city at night. I was getting hungry at this stage and I asked her to find me somewhere to eat. No problem. She found me a very nice little all-night bistro just outside Cherbourg.

I arrived home a short while ago. I never did pass through the village. My confidence in technology is a little shaken. When we head off on the holiday, I think I'll use a map.

NOSTALGIA ISN'T WHAT IT USED TO BE

So what kind of holiday did I have? A quiet one.

It was a very nice hotel. For some strange reason it was full of people from Norn Iron (for you foreigners, that's Northern Ireland, but that's the way they pronounce it and who am I to argue?). Maybe they were all trying to escape their new smoking ban? We were all of a respectable age. There were a few children in their thirties, but they behaved themselves.

On the first night, when the locals had been thrown out, about thirty of us got a little merry and started on about the good old days. Someone put some Beatles on the CD player and someone else brought out a huge stash of Mary Jane and soon the entire pub was awash with nostalgia and the smell of pot.

Do you honestly think that we older folk spend our time moaning about arthritis and pretending we can't hear anything? That's just an act to get you younger folk to run around and fetch and carry for us. We know how to enjoy ourselves once you are in bed.

I think it was Megan from Belfast who was the first to get carried away, in the middle of *Strawberry Fields*. Off came the clothes and the next thing we were celebrating the 1960s in style. Anyone who wasn't pissed was high. And anyone who wasn't high was pissed. And a few of us were both.

The following morning was a bit confusing, as quite a few woke up in strange bedrooms and had trouble finding the breakfast room. No one minded because we all put it down to failing memory (hah!).

As the young people were around again, we had to revert to the walking sticks and the limps and the hard-of-hearing act, but we didn't mind. We had the evening to look forward to again.

You young people haven't a clue how to enjoy yourselves.

HOW TO IMPROVE YOUR AIM IN LIFE

I had a phone call from my doctor yesterday. A phone call from the doctor is a bit like seeing two policemen on your doorstep, or getting a telegram (though that doesn't happen much these days). All sorts of thoughts flash through your mind.

Had I forgotten to pay a bill?

Did he finally get the results of the blood test he took five years ago?

Was I to be nominated for 'Hypochondriac of the Year'?

Had I run over his dog again?

So I called down to the surgery.

Doc and I get on very well. We have the same warped sense of humour. He can even accurately predict which of my bits is likely to fall off next. I'd go for a pint with him, but it's hard to be chatty with a bloke who has had his finger up your arse.

'What's up, Doc?' says I in my best Bugs Bunny style.

'I'm concerned,' says he. 'I think it is time we changed your medication. I'm worried about some side effects.'

'Oh?' says I, not knowing what else to say.

'I was up by the lakes over the weekend and I saw you taking pot shots at the tourists again.'

'Ah!' says I. 'You think maybe my medication isn't calming me enough? Should I be on something stronger?'

'No. It's not that. I couldn't help but notice that you missed a couple of times, which isn't like you. I think the medication might be making your hands shake a bit.'

I was very relieved. I thought he was going to tell me that the tablets might turn my pee green or something nasty like that. So he has put me on a different lot. He says it will take a few weeks to completely remove that twitch in the hand. Just in time for the height of the tourist season.

I told you he's a nice bloke.

THELMA AND LOUISE, IRISH STYLE

I went down to the village yesterday for a coffee.

I could have had one at home but Herself wanted to go shopping, so Sandy and I sat in the rain and the hot sun (we have very strange weather here) and watched the world go by. The village was packed with people looking for directions.

Do these knob-heads decide, 'Oh look, it's a nice day. Let's go out and get lost'? Once they have decided where they are going, why can't they work out how to get there? The local shopkeepers spend more time giving directions than they do trading. As you probably know, I get my revenge by sending them all up to the bogs where they can get totally lost.

Yesterday though, I was nearly caught out. I was stopped by a bloke driving a souped-up Golf that had purple lights underneath and made a noise like a Boeing 747 on full take-off power. I hate them. But this bloke actually wanted to know the way to the bogs! I had to think quickly.

'Carry on this road,' says I, 'and take the fourth turn to

the right. You can't miss it. It has an old ruined cottage on the corner.'

He thanked me and roared off like he was contesting the Round Ireland Rally.

That road I directed him to is a nice little road. It is quite straight for a bit and then there is a slight bend. Immediately past that bend the road ends suddenly at the top of a 200-foot cliff into a quarry. There's no warning. You've seen *Thelma and Louise*? Like that!

I wonder if he stopped in time?

THE NIGHT I DIED, BUT DIDN'T

We had a winter storm last night. I don't remember the weatherman saying anything about storms. But then I didn't see the weather forecast.

Anyway, we were sitting watching something really crap on television with the volume turned up so we could hear it over the wind. Herself chose the programme. Next thing – pop – I was sitting in darkness and silence.

I thought for a moment I had died (it was a *very* bad programme), or that maybe I had gone blind and deaf simultaneously. But then I heard a quiet 'fuck' from out of the dark, so I knew the electricity had gone.

Being country dwellers, we always have plenty of candles and an oil lamp so I fired them up. Now, candles and oil lamps don't really give enough light to read by. Not with our sight anyway. So we had to talk. We discussed going to bed, but we decided against it, as we couldn't read there either.

Herself was all wired up because she had blogged yesterday for the first time in months and was in a fierce communicative mood. We decided to phone a neighbour to see if he was OK. He wasn't really pleased at being woken in the dark to be told there was a power cut. We told him it was too early for sleep (it was only one in the morning) and hung up.

We then decided to ring all our friends who we hadn't spoken to in a long time. It seemed a nice friendly thing to do. I rang one elderly relative to ask if she had died yet. She said she hadn't but thanked me for asking. I rang another friend about some money I owed him. I won't tell you where he told me to stick my money, but that's another debt I can forget about.

For some reason, people weren't very talkative, so we got tired of that and went to bed in the end.

This morning, the power was still off. And sod's law kicked in and I woke early. So I sat in the cold and drank water. (Why is a house always colder during a power cut, even when you don't have heating?) For once, all the trees are still standing, which is very unusual. But then I haven't walked around the estate yet.

There were quite a few messages on our answering service, as we'd switched the phone off last night. They weren't very nice messages for some reason.

The power came back at half nine. I knew because the house suddenly got warmer. Now I am in the process of catching up on all the cups of tea I missed out on. Then I think I'll have a nap.

NEIGHBOURS

One of my neighbours has decided to knock his house down. Quite why he's doing it, I'm not sure. Maybe he doesn't like the wallpaper? I offered to do it for him, because I have some spare Semtex left over from last Hallowe'en. But he said no.

Anyway, a van load of Poles arrived yesterday along with a lorry load of poles. The Poles erected the poles around the house and started work. I don't think my neighbour had expected them to work so quickly and he had to move out. Fast.

A lorry arrived today to cart away the remains. There is no way they could get into the driveway so they parked the lorry in the lane and used one of those grab things to scoop the rubble onto the lorry. The only snag was that the lorry was the precise width of the lane, so no one could get past it. Not even on foot. And there was a lot of rubble to shift, so it was there a long time.

My doorbell started ringing.

'I can't get home. Can you ask them to move the lorry please?'

'But that lorry has nothing to do with me,' says I.

'I know, but they won't talk to me. Maybe they'll talk to you?'

'No. They won't talk to me,' says I. I didn't say that this morning the Poles had all been sitting in a circle eating their breakfast. Our Sandy got out, went over into the middle of the circle and did a huge dump in front of them all. This was a bit embarrassing for me, and very strange as our Sandy is usually very discreet. Maybe she doesn't like Poles?

'Can I take a short cut through your field?'

'No. Go sit in your car and be patient!'

This happened twice. Different people. And these people get their oil delivered or whatever and they block the lane, but I don't complain. People are so damned impatient these days.

What I don't understand though is that whenever something goes wrong in this area, people always blame me. Why?

SREDLIUB

I mentioned how the neighbours had knocked down their house. The builders have been working like the clappers all week. You'd know they weren't Irish.

There are two of them. I don't know what nationality they are, but the always give me a friendly wave as I patrol my boundaries. They used to stop for meal breaks, but since our Sandy did a dump on their breakfast table, they don't even do that any more.

They start work every morning at seven. Yesterday, they were working until midnight, non-stop. That's seventeen hours. I'd love to see an Irish builder do that! And they were back this morning at seven.

They caused mayhem yesterday, as they had a stream of huge lorries delivering fresh concrete. None of the lorries could enter the land so they blocked the lane while the concrete was trucked in bit by bit. The other neighbours were not best pleased.

I know how they do it though. I know where they get their stamina from. They have a little dumper truck and that's what gave them away. All day yesterday it was going beep beep beep. Which meant they were driving it backwards. So that's it. They do *everything* backwards.

It makes sense when you think about it. If you go backwards then you end up earlier than when you started. And you are not as tired, because you are now only beginning the job. Very clever. I'd love to talk to Einstein about it, but he isn't around at the moment.

They're out there beavering away at the moment in the pissing rain. I checked, and, yes, they are still going backwards. And the work is coming on at a fierce rate. But they must have realised that the beep beep beep was a bit of a giveaway, because they switched it off yesterday and haven't switched it on again.

But I know their secret. I'm not stupid.

WAITING

Dear God,

I am writing to you in desperation.

I have led a good life. I have never done anyone any harm (apart from a couple of tourists, but they don't count) and treat all your creation with great respect. What have I done to annoy you? Are you having a laugh? Is all this crap weather a wee joke? If so, then I think your humour is a little warped. You must realise that a joke can wear thin. And this joke has frankly gone totally anorexic.

I completely understand if this is the start of a biblical flood. The world has gone to the dogs and maybe a flood is a good idea. It worked before. But last time you at least had the courtesy to tell Noah in advance. If it is a biblical flood, then at least warn me so that I can start rounding up a few animals. Just in case, I have started construction on the ark and it's coming on quite well. I have made provision for all the animals (except wasps, tourists and politicians).

Could you please stop faffing about. Could you please tell me if this is the flood, or is this just your warped humour? Even better – could you please give us a bit of summer?

Yours in dampness,
Grandad.

P.S. That lightning bolt that just hit my favourite tree wasn't funny either.

NEW POLICY FOR TOURISTS

I went to the village this afternoon. I was sitting outside the coffee shop, enjoying my coffee and a puff on the pipe when I saw a couple of tourists. They were prime targets. Not only did they look lost, but one of them was a SOTH (Sunglasses on the Head for future reference). I was just lining up the shot, when they caught me by surprise. They called me over!

I crossed the road to see what they wanted. Luckily they didn't notice the rifle. Apparently they wanted someone to photograph them. So I did. I shot them with their own camera, so to speak. They were delighted and were very grateful. They then asked for directions …

Now I felt a bit sorry for them. I was tempted to send them up to the bogs, but it's getting quite crowded up there. And anyway, they were a nice couple. So I told them I was a stranger to the area, and they would be better off asking directions in the local supermarket.

None of the staff in the local supermarket speak English! They can't find where the pipe tobacco is, let alone where the local tourist attractions are. I went back to my coffee and waited to see which direction my friends ended up taking. They came out of the supermarket and headed off on the wrong road, of course.

So. No more bog. From now on, I'm going to send everyone into the supermarket. I can take bets with myself as to which road out of the village they'll take. It's like a lottery. It's much more fun.

THE DECLINE OF THE VILLAGE

I went down to the village again for coffee yesterday. This is getting to be a habit.

As I sat in the sun, supped my coffee and puffed the pipe with Sandy sitting at my feet, I contemplated village life. When I first moved here (long before most of you were born), it was just a little country village. I was treated as a 'blow-in' at first and was tolerated with politeness. It was a close-knit community where everyone knew everyone else and outsiders were treated with a little suspicion.

I moved away for some years, without losing my village connections, and am back again. The place has changed. The village is much the same, but houses are springing up in the surrounding area. The new 'blow-ins' are all terribly impressed to be living the village life, but they don't understand what village life is. Their community consists of the golf club or the tennis club. They sit in the village and arrange dinner parties (at the top of their voices so that we are in no doubt what they are talking about) on their mobile phones. Of course, they all drive SUVs. They talk (again, as loudly as possible) how they are *just* back from Thailand and *can't wait* to get to Marbella next month.

The village is infested with affluenza.

Those of us from 'the old days' are now firm friends. We are sticking together like animals in a dwindling clump of rainforest. We know our days are numbered.

ODDS AND ENDS

'Are you going down to the village today?' says Herself.

'Nah. I'm not going out at all today. I have a bad feeling.'

'What do you mean, feeling?'

'I just know something very bad is going to happen if I go out.'

'Like what?'

'I just know that if I drive down to the village I am going to be killed.'

'What?'

'If I drive today, I am going to come to the crossroads. There will be a woman driving a BMW on the other road. She will be talking on her mobile and, as she comes to the crossroads, she will drop her lipstick that she's applying using the rear-view mirror. She will bend down to pick it up and will drive straight past the stop sign and into me. I'll be pushed into the path of an oncoming bus and will be mangled against the wall. Dead. Or a vegetable for the rest of my life.'

'That's stupid.'

'Why? It could happen.'

'But the odds on that happening are ridiculously small. One in a thousand. Or more like one in a million.'

'But it could happen!'

'Look,' says Herself patiently, 'with those odds, it just isn't going to happen. Forget about it. You have a higher chance of being struck by lightning.'

'I suppose you're right. What did you want in the village anyway?'

'I wanted to buy a lottery ticket.'

COUNT YOUR BLESSINGS

Herself and her damned lottery ticket! The numbers came up and my heart sank. What am I supposed to do with

€16,000,000? That is a stupid amount of money. Monopoly money.

What I'm dreading is the beggars and the begging letters. All those people whinging and whining about how hard up they are and could I spare a few bob to help them on their way. Damned relatives!

Of course I'll be the toast of the bar. Everyone will expect me to buy the drinks. Which I will, because I don't want to appear mean. So I'll become a mobile ATM, and nothing more. I will doubtless have hundreds of new 'friends' fawning all over me, saying how great I am, when all they want is the handout. I will lose my old friends, because I will be constantly talking about my new lifestyle, which isn't the old me.

Money changes people. I have seen it. It changes them for the worse. They become lonely and isolated. People don't like them any more for what they are, but rather for what they have. The only friends they have are the ones they buy. Too much money, and you know the price of everything and the value of nothing.

Herself and I had to save for holidays. Meals out were a treat. We couldn't afford to go to exotic places and could only dream. Now we can afford to go out every night. We can afford to go anywhere, for as long as we like. Nothing will be special any more. We won't appreciate the treats, because they will be mundane.

That ticket is a curse. It will remove any incentive to strive. In fact, I'm going out now. I'm going to give it to the first passing motorist who stops. Poor bastard.

NEAT AND TIDY

The other day that I bought Herself a Dyson. While I was out, I thought I'd buy myself a little gift too.

We have this crazy setup where we are encouraged to install wood burning stoves (eco-friendly), but are outlawed from burning wood in the garden (eco-unfriendly). And my humble little estate is of an age where, instead of planting things, it's a constant battle to keep plants in check. So I spend a lot of time hacking at things and cutting branches. And, of course, the weather does a good job too. So I have ended up with a massive pile of old branches. And I'm not allowed to burn them.

I went into the hardware shop and toddled over to the gardening section. I found an assistant (that took half an hour).

'Do you sell munchers?' says I.

'Munchers?' says he. 'Oh! You mean shredders?'

He brought me down to one of those hidden areas that always seem to contain whatever I'm looking for. There were a couple of munchers there and they looked impressive. The salesman started prattling on about how efficient they were and how powerful. It occurred to me that between manufacture, transportation and running costs, these beasts probably had a massive eco-footprint compared to a piddly bonfire, but I let that pass. He also raved about the safety features. He pointed out that there was a special yoke at the top to stop you accidentally putting your hand in.

'Suppose I left that yoke off?' says I.

'That would be very dangerous.' He looked at me like I were a fool.

'Would it grind up my arm?'

He just looked at me. But I'm patient.

'A simple question,' says I. 'Would I be able to put, say, a severed leg through it?'

He turned very green and fainted. Young people these days have no backbone. I bought it anyway and towed it home.

I've been playing with it for a few days now. It's brilliant. It chews up everything. The mountain of branches is gone. And I discovered in the manual that it is great for shredding paper too. Better and better. I have quite a few ~~invoices from arms dealers~~ old bank statements that I didn't want to put in the bin so in they went.

So happy days are here again. Herself spends the day vacuuming the house and I spend the day ~~destroying evidence~~ making compost.

PROS AND CONS

I find as I get older, things are changing. Some changes are for the better and some for the worse. But each change in its own way has its pros and cons.

Sleep

My sleep has become very erratic. I usually go to sleep at the same time each night, but wake up at different times. I set the alarm for nine (old habits die hard), but it rarely goes off. Usually I wake anywhere between five o'clock and one minute to nine (I have a very accurate body clock!).

Pros:
- I get to see the sun rise and hear the dawn chorus
- I get nice long days

Cons:
- I end up sleeping most of the day, wasting all that hard won time

Memory

I've mentioned this often. Short-term is getting terrible. Long-term is improving.

Pros:
- We can watch the same film time and time again
- Great excuse for getting out of things

Cons:
- Can never find things

Flatulence

I don't know if this is old age or diet, but it's on the increase

Pros:
- Great for entertaining small boys
- Great for annoying Herself

Cons:
- Can be embarrassing at funerals

- Terrible when Herself retaliates

Pension

A wage for work you don't have to do any more.

Pros:
- Regular
- Can't get docked if you take time off

Cons:
- Can't earn overtime
- If money runs short, you have to rob the post office again

Mood

Old age and irritation seem to go together. *Grumpy Old Men/Women* is not just a television programme.

Pros:
- You get better service as it's expected that you'll complain
- Great satisfaction at tearing strips off people

Cons:
- Everything is fucking irritating

Flirting

At my age, I can flirt outrageously. Women know I'm not a threat, as I'm only an old fart.

Pros:
- Makes me feel younger
- Sometimes find women who like old farts

Cons:
- None

Grandparenthood

Pros:
- All the joys of children without the pain or expense
- Watching your offspring repeating all the things they used to complain about
- Instant eviction of children if you get tired or bored

Cons:
- Automatically adds twenty years to your age overnight
- Perceived as a built in babysitter

There are many others, but the memory has kicked in (out) again. See above.

IN THE HEAT OF THE MOMENT

We have just had a heat wave. It lasted all day Tuesday.

Ron drove over on Tuesday evening and we decided to go hunting. The fine weather brings out the tourists. It was a beautiful evening, and the tourists were grazing up and down the forest tracks. A perfect evening.

I got off a lovely shot. A clean kill. Unfortunately, the bullet passed through, ricocheted off a rock and I shot Ron as well. Two birds with one stone, as it were.

Ron tried to shoot me back, but couldn't. Poor bastard was probably in agony. But he didn't have to make such a fuss over it. He's a bit of a mammy's boy at heart. And who needs that many fingers anyway?

I was all on for continuing the hunt but Ron's yelling had alerted them all. Anyway he was bleeding all over the place while he looked for his missing fingers. So I bundled him in the car and brought him to the nearest bus stop, so he could get himself to hospital. It was the least I could do, I suppose. I would have brought him the whole way, but I wanted to get home to see the weather forecast.

I rang the hospital today. They said they didn't know what his condition was. Apparently he's still in the waiting room. They told me to ring back in a month's time. They might have dealt with him by then.

AN EXPLANATION

There has been some concern and confusion about my references to shooting tourists. I had better explain.

Back in the early 1980s the Irish Tourist Board launched a campaign advertising the beauty and friendliness of Ireland as a tourist destination. Unfortunately, they were somewhat over-zealous and this resulted in a tourist influx which was unprecedented. Within months, our roads were crowded, our scenic spots couldn't be seen for the crowds and there was no accommodation left.

This left the Irish Tourist Board and the Irish government in an embarrassing position. They couldn't ask people not to visit, but yet the infrastructure was not in place to cope with the influx.

What was worse, some of the visitors decided that Ireland was such a beautiful place that they would settle here. This pushed land prices up to an extent that local residents were unable to live there any more.

The solution arrived at was to cull the tourists. Seal culling had led to a lot of adverse publicity for Canada, and it was therefore decided that tourist culling should be kept as quiet as possible. Tourist culling was heavily regulated from the outset. It is a licensed sport, and the rules are strict. The culling of the young is prohibited, as is the culling of fertile females. A kill must be as clean as possible. We didn't want photographs of the Irish clubbing baby tourists to death on blood soaked beaches. I think the Canadians will testify to the undesirability of that.

Since then, tourist culling has become a popular sport. It is carried out in most parts of Ireland, though incidents are rare in the major cities, because of the danger to locals. It is run on a points system, with maximum points going to a cull of tourists who are obviously contemplating buying land. It is a complex system of scoring, which I won't go into now.

There have been attempts to outlaw the sport in recent years, as people are arguing that we now have the road and hotel infrastructure. However, we who enjoy the sport have taken the same line as the fox hunters in the UK – namely that it is now a rural tradition and that there is no cruelty involved.

I'M OLDER THAN I LOOK AND I'M YOUNGER THAN I FEEL

I wrote an article on the pros and cons of growing old. Some people seemed a little surprised that I was so happy about it. People are saying that growing old sounds like fun. It is.

When I was young, I was immortal. I was going to live forever. But one of the little signs of ageing is that you suddenly realise that this isn't true. My time is finite. One of these days or years, God (or whoever) is going to come barrelling along my little road in a SUV and run me over. And that will be it.

So I am savouring every day. And I'm sorry I didn't savour every day when I was younger. According to the Real Age clock, I have another thirty years to go yet!! But I am going to live each and every day.

I have learned a lot on my path through life. I have learned to have confidence in myself. I have learned that other people's opinions of me don't matter. I can wander down to the village in my slippers, or speak in front of a large crowd. I can type immature absurdities in my blog. If people don't like what I do or what I have to say then I don't care. This is me. Provided I don't actually do anything offensive, I can do what I like. I am what I am.

I try to lead what I would call a moral life. I do unto others as I would have them do unto me. I bear no ill will towards anyone. Enemies are a waste of energy and life. Friends are precious.

In some ways, I have had a hard life. I have known days where I have searched down the back of cushions for a few coins so I can buy a loaf of bread. I have spent years in jobs that I hated, where the work was hard and the pay was poor. I have seen the death of both my parents and my sister. I have known worry and pain. But you can't really appreciate the sunshine unless you have felt the cold rain.

I am free now. I am retired, but I carry on working. I work because I enjoy it. I can do the work I want to do. I earn money for the little extras in life, not because the mortgage demands it. I have learned that money is a preoccupation that is rotting society. People are obsessed with it. They think it is the key to happiness. They are wrong. The key to happiness is peace of mind.

I am blessed with a happy family. I have had thirty-something years of marriage and we are very happy. We have a daughter who is beautiful, intelligent and very witty. We have two grandchildren who are the real sunshine in our lives.

I earn a lot less now than I did ten years ago. I demand less than I did ten years ago. To me, happiness is not a skiing holiday every winter and a fortnight in the sun every summer. To me happiness is watching a dove sunbathing on the lawn, or a grandchild's laughter.

Above all, I act my age. I am thirty(ish). My passport will say otherwise, as will the aches in the joints, but they are just my body getting a bit rusty. But my age changes. Sometimes, when I play with my granddaughter, I am a five-year-old. But if my granddaughter bumps her head and needs a cuddle, I am a sixty-year-old grandad. That is nice too.

Now that I'm retired, I'm not going to take up bridge or bowls. I'm not going to join any seniors' clubs. I don't go to the pensioners' Christmas dinner (as I'm entitled to) in my old place of work. That's for old people. I'm going to carry on being a thirty-year-old. For the rest of my life. They can carve that on my gravestone: 'Here lies an old man, who died age thirty'.

YOUR THREE MINUTES ARE UP

It's amazing how much we take for granted these days.

Herself went to the dentist during the week. She got a prescription for antibiotics which violently disagreed with her. So we rang the dentist and he promptly faxed through a different prescription. I was able to nip down and get her the new medication. All in the space of less than half an hour.

Just think about it. Not many years ago, I could have phoned the dentist, but I then would have had to drive over to collect the prescription (a long journey) and by the time I got back the chemist would have been closed. Or else he could have posted it, which would have taken even longer.

If I want cash at any time of day or night (you never know when you might need the odd €50 at 3 a.m.!) I can nip down to the ATM and withdraw that cash. Not that long ago, if you needed cash, you had to go to the bank and withdraw it. And the banks had very awkward opening hours. It usually meant taking time off work. So, if you wanted to go on the batter on a Saturday night you had to make sure you had enough cash in your pocket or you were done for. Pubs and shops didn't take Laser cards (they hadn't been invented) and might take a cheque if you had your passport, a valid cheque card and were closely related to the owner of the establishment.

If I want to phone someone, it doesn't matter where I am, I just whip a tiny box out of my pocket and phone them. In the old days, it would have meant a hunt around for a phone box (80% of which were probably vandalised) and then I had to pray I had the right change.

If I want to talk to my blogging friends in America or Australia, I just plug in my microphone and call them on Skype. Free! In the old days, it would have meant booking a call with the exchange operator. They would then give you a time to call. Even then, when you were making the call, and having a chat, the operator would cut in and tell you that another three minutes were up, and did you wish to continue? And it would cost a fortune for each extra three minutes.

For those of you who have grown up in the modern world of mobile phones, the Internet and the World Wide Web, it must seem like they were around forever. They weren't. They seemed to descend overnight, and they changed the world radically. Even now, I find it very strange that as I type these words, they will shortly be visible in just about every country in the world, for anyone who cares to read them.

It's no wonder I'm getting paranoid about my spelling and grammar.

SIDE EFFECTS

One of the drags of getting old is that you have to start taking medication.

Every night I have to take a big red pill. This pill has side effects – it causes disorientation and makes me walk in circles.

- To counteract that I take another pill. This pill has side effects – it causes hormone imbalance and makes me grow boobs.
- To counteract that I take another pill. This pill has side effects – it causes erectile function and gives me a permanent stiffy.
- To counteract that I take another pill. This pill has side effects – it causes visual impairment and gives me a terrible squint.
- To counteract that I take another pill. This pill has side effects – it causes aggression and makes me want to kill everyone.
- To counteract that I take another pill. This pill has side effects – it makes my skin turn green.
- To counteract that I take the big red pill.

PLEASE PHONE ME SO I CAN SCREW YOU

Last night I got bored with making obscene phonecalls. So I decided, against my principles, to watch television.

I checked what was on the various channels. RTÉ 1, RTÉ 2, TV3, TG4, BBC2 and Channel 4 were all showing films I had either seen before or didn't want to see. That left BBC1 and ITV. BBC1 – *Dance X*. ITV – *The X Factor*. Jayzus!

What is it with these inane knockout shows on television? They get a bunch of nonentities and wannabe celebrities (everyone apparently wants to be a 'celebrity' these days) and get them to make total fools of themselves for our 'entertainment'. They are the most boring thing ever invented. *Big Brother*; *You're a Star*; *Celebrity Castaway* – they are all the same.

One thing they all have in common. They all want you to phone in your vote. Now that's clever. Not only do they get their advertising fees, but they get you poor saps to fund them too with your premium phone costs. They make millions out of convincing brainless idiots to vote. How do you think *Who Wants to be a Millionaire* is funded? Even *Questions and Answers* on RTÉ is getting in on the act. And ITV News! The television companies have discovered that there is big money to be made by screwing the public. And the public love to be screwed.

I never watch any programme that invites phone calls from the public. They are always to premium lines. At least I can make my obscene phone calls for nothing.

We ended up watching *Legends of the Fall*. It was good. I like Anthony Hopkins. It was on TCM. The last refuge of the desperate.

A ROSE BY ANY OTHER NAME

I was exposed to the most horrendous torture last night.

I managed to grab the TV listings and sit on them. But I had to go for a pee. Herself grabbed the listings while I was out of the room. By the time I got back, she had discovered that *The Rose of Tralee* was on. Now you know why I was sitting on the listings.

I pleaded. I begged. I threatened. But she switched over anyway. She had the remote control and the frying pan, so it was out of my hands.

The Rose of Tralee is car-crash television at its best (or worst). You find yourself covering your eyes and then peeking through your fingers. It's like the Eurovision, but without Terry Wogan to take the piss out of it. And it goes on, and on, and on, and on.

We saw the second half of the first part last night. Herself has booked it for tonight because she says there is nothing else on. I think I'll stay out in the kitchen and extract my teeth with the pliers.

What gets me is that the girls are all exactly the same. Somewhere in China, there is a factory churning them out (presumably with a lethal lead content). They try to disguise that they are different by giving them different accents (and the American ones have to say 'so, like' every ten seconds) but the formula gives them away.

- They all do Irish dancing.
- They all think the best thing that has ever happened to them is getting to the finals.

- They all wanted to be contestants when they watched the programme as children.
- They are all pursuing (or about to pursue) incredibly rewarding careers.
- If they are not Irish, they are there because their great-great-grandfather was deported for stealing turnips.
- They all designed or made their dresses.
- None of them want to win. Being there is enough.

I'm waiting for the first girl to admit that she was thrown out of school in first year and that she has been a pole dancer since she was sixteen to support the five kids (Jacinta, Brittney, Jason, Brad and Mercedes). She'll tell Ray D'Arcy to fuck off because he's asking boring questions. For her talent spot she'll sing a song she composed herself about her court appearances. None of her family will be in the audience, because they couldn't get temporary release. She will finally flounce off the stage taking all the trophies with her (hidden under the blanket in Jacinta's pram).

Now there's a girl that represents modern Ireland!

MY APOLOGIES

I would like to apologise to my Irish readers for the current spell of unseasonable fine weather. I know Irish summers should be cold and damp with frequent showers with the occasional flash flood, tornado or hurricane. But for the last few days, it has been warm (some might even say hot?) and sunny. I'm sorry about this.

You see, I'm to blame. I have always had this weird knack of being able to control the weather. If I buy a pair of sunglasses, we don't see the sun for months. If I buy a new pair of windscreen wipers for the car, then the rain vanishes. They have to introduce hosepipe bans and the entire population of Galway nearly dies of thirst.

I have thought about hiring myself out. If you are suffering from severe flooding, I will move there and buy a boat. You are guaranteed to be gasping for water within days. If you are suffering from severe heat, I will move there and buy some suntan lotion. You will soon forget what the sun looks like.

This latest strange sunny weather is caused by my old flooring. I wanted to break up the mountain of scrap timber into kindling, and I discovered that if it is damp, then the laminate peels off easily (it is, after all, extremely high quality flooring!). So I put the whole lot into the garden to get damp. And that is when the fine weather started.

If this goes on much longer, I may throw the floor into the pond and let it get damp that way.

Then we can get back to the miserable grey damp weather that we know and love so well.

SMOKING MAKES YOU LIVE LONGER

Fact.

Studies by eminent psychologists show that happiness

increases your lifespan. Apparently, a happy, positive person can expect to live ten years longer.

Now, they claim smoking can knock five years off your life, though they don't mention the figures for pipe smoking. So if I quit the pipe, I am going to be miserable, because I enjoy it and would miss it. That's ten years gone. I have decided not to quit, so that makes me happy and content. My ten years are back. Smoking is possibly going to knock five years off that, but I'm still five years in profit.

Apparently (and I quote) *'In terms of living longer and healthier, positive feelings are more important than body mass, smoking and exercise'*. So I'm going to light up my pipe now and relax in my armchair. In doing so, I am adding five years to my lifespan.

QED.

MY LOVING DAUGHTER

I am getting concerned.

Some time ago, K8 and TAT started leaving stuff here 'for storage'. First it was a log burner. That was followed by a fridge, a patio heater, a gas cylinder and various other bits and pieces. We have also somehow inherited a trampoline and an inflatable children's pool. Now TAT has left their computer here. And that is *very* dear to his heart. He can't live without his games.

K8 has somehow acquired a key to the house and is insisting that I park permanently in the lane, in case they call. I'm also starting to get their post. And phone calls. The calls for K8 are OK, but the calls for TAT are rather worrying ('Tell TAT that the job is on for Tuesday night' or 'Tell TAT that the shipment is arriving in Dingle Bay'. They never leave a name or a number.)

They called again on Sunday. TAT rewired my office in a strange way, so that his equipment works but mine doesn't. K8 cooked us a *beautiful* barbecue that was like nothing I have ever tasted before. She wouldn't say what the meat was (but come to think of it, I haven't seen the neighbour's cat since!). Then she went off and measured all the windows.

This morning we had a couple of strange phone calls. The first was from a builder who wants to convert our garage into a games room. The second was from a rather cranky woman in the 'Shangri La' retirement home in Reykjavik, in Iceland about a lifetime booking (?). Both callers hung up when they realised that K8 wasn't here.

I am extremely honoured that K8 and TAT want to give me all their furniture and stuff and even their precious computer. It is very generous of them. They are lovely kids. But why do they want to book themselves into an old folk's home in Iceland? I'll never understand my daughter. I'm a bit concerned for her.

IF IT AIN'T BROKE - FIX IT

This morning, I did what I do most mornings. I made myself a cuppa, and sat down with the laptop, to check my mail.

'Server Not Found'. Bugger!!
Went to check a website or two.
'Page cannot be loaded'. Double bugger!!

I tried various things, but couldn't get connected. Now, it's still early in the morning so I'm not really thinking straight. I jump to the natural conclusion that my broadband has failed. Now this means a long phone call with my provider, where I will try to get my message through to someone who hasn't a word of English. But I ring them anyway.

So I go through the usual hoops of pressing different numbers and listening to musak and ads and things and eventually get through to a real person. Foreign, of course, but a reasonable command of the language. I give him my details and explain that I have no service.

I have one of those cordless phones, and to while away the time I tend to wander around the place. I wandered over to my main PC (I am a man of the modern world – PCs all over the place!) and switched it on.

While I am telling this bloke that my service is down, the main PC starts downloading mail. All the usual penis enlargements start arriving in my inbox. Shit!

I nip back to the laptop and it is still dead. I realise then that somehow the wireless button thingy is not lit. Somehow, it got switched off. I switched it on, and there was my connection. Double shit!

And all this time, the bloke on the phone is protesting that he can find nothing wrong with my connection and I am insisting that I can't connect. So what do I do now? If I admit it is my fault, then I will lose credibility and they will laugh at me and never take me seriously again. The bloke then starts complaining that he can see traffic on my sector going to my connection. So I tell him that's impossible.

'There's no connection,' I said, 'so how can there be traffic?'

I demanded to speak to a supervisor. The supervisors there never speak to anyone (I don't think they have any) so I knew I was safe. He started to panic. He started pressing buttons all over the place. I could hear his keyboard clacking like mad.

'There!' I shouted. 'Whatever you just did brought my service back!'

'But I did not do anything,' he replied.

'Yes you did,' I said, 'and my service is now fine. Thank you very much. You have been a great help and I'm going to write to the management and tell them how good you are.'

I hung up. I'm sure I have made him feel good. He feels he has accomplished something and has received a verbal pat on the back. The call wasn't a waste of time.

Now I have to wade through the penis enlargements, and see if any of them are any good.

GOOD THINGS COME IN SMALL PARCELS

I bought my first car in 1972. It was an Austin Mini and was clapped out when I got it. It was red, which was great, because when the paint flaked off, the rust underneath was the same colour.

Few of you will remember the first Minis. They had a few distinctive features. One was that to start the car, you turned the key in the ignition and then pressed a button on the floor to actually start the motor. The other was the windows. They didn't wind down, they slid sideways.

My Mini was well ventilated. In fact, if you pulled the passenger floor mat back, you could watch the road passing underneath. And it was always damp inside, so I grew a couple of beautiful ferns in the passenger door. Actually, I didn't plant them – they just appeared.

It was a bit of a squeeze driving that car because I'm over 6 foot tall, but I didn't mind that. It had a personality of its own. Lots of things never really worked properly. The heating never worked, and the breaks used to fail on a regular basis. On one occasion, I was pissed out of my mind and the breaks decided to fail completely just as the lights ahead changed red. That car had a wicked sense of timing. I smacked into the car in front in an explosion of glass and rust. The car in front wasn't damaged as the rust had taken all the damage. I had to get a taxi home. That cost more than the car was worth.

I had long hair in those days, and the police took great delight in stopping me to examine the car. I used to get away with it, as the tyres looked good and the tax and insurance (£50!) were always up to date. On one occasion I actually got a summons: 'no illumination on my rear identification plate'. I went to court. The judge was in foul mood. All the cases before me were for similar trivial offences and as the plaintiffs' excuses got more frantic, so the fines increased. By the time he got around to me, the fines were running at around the £100 mark.

'What's your excuse?' the judge roared at me.

'None,' I said, 'I knew it was broken but didn't think it was that important. I was going to get it fixed the next time I was in town.'

'At last,' he shouted, 'a bit of honesty! Fined £5.'

I loved that car. It was always breaking down, but the mechanics were so simple it was very easy to fix at the side of the road. We had many very happy adventures together.

One frosty morning I went to go to work. I pressed the floor button to start the engine. There was a loud thump from the front, that didn't sound healthy. I got out and opened the bonnet. The engine had fallen out and was sitting sadly on the ground between the wheels. I knew its time had come.

I went and bought myself another Mini. But it wasn't the same.

HOW TO DISEMBOWEL A BUS

I try to lead a quiet life. Somehow the gods conspire against this, and keep throwing weird things at me.

Last night, at around half eleven, I was sitting quietly contemplating the sounds of the night and the roar of the buses drag racing up and down the main road. A bus came roaring along in second gear and suddenly there was a loud bang and total silence. It was if someone had pressed the mute button. It was the total silence that unnerved me, because double-decker buses don't just suddenly disappear.

I sauntered out to see what had happened and there was the bus, parked in the middle of the road (on a sharp bend). For about 50 feet behind it, the road was covered in the contents of its engine. There were huge gears and universal joints. There were shards of broken cast iron. There was a bit of a drive shaft that was the size of a small tree trunk. And there was diesel fuel flowing down the road in a small flood. There was also a rather bemused looking bus driver, sitting in his cab, pressing buttons and things.

'I don't think that will do much good,' says I.

'I think you're right,' says he, 'there seems to be something up with the engine. All the warning lights are on red.'

I asked if there was a warning light to say that his engine and gearbox were missing and he admitted there wasn't. So I told him that they were scattered down the road behind him. He got out and looked.

'Fuck,' says he.

'That about describes it,' says I.

So we rang the garage and we rang the police, because the road was nearly blocked and the river of diesel was flowing unabated. There was also a huge hole, about 15 foot deep in the road, that hadn't been there earlier in the day. I realised it was probably one of my old tourist-bus traps that I'd forgotten about that had suddenly sprung. I didn't mention that.

So we waited for the tow truck and the engineers and the police. We got very pally. I learned a lot about buses. Did you know that they removed all the Imp buses because they kept going on fire? Do you know that there are virtually no single-deckers left? I bet you didn't know that every single bus has nine high definition video cameras on board that record everything that goes on?

We had great fun waving down drunken drivers to stop them driving into the hole or skidding on the fuel or hitting any of the debris.

All the diesel fuel nicely poured into an Eircom manhole that was conveniently placed. Next time an Eircom technician opens a junction box down in the village, he is going to be swept away in a flood of diesel.

Eventually, a convoy of tow trucks and buses arrived. It was an hour after we called them. They were out there all night cleaning up the mess. We're still waiting on the police.

WHEREFORE ART THOU, RON?

I went for a pint last night. The place was full of tourists and they seemed to have driven the regulars away. I blame the sunshine.

Anyway, I sat outside on the bonnet of a brand new Land Rover Discovery that was illegally (and very badly) parked outside the pub, and enjoyed my pipe and pint as the evening settled in. I was idly doodling on the paintwork of the Discovery with my car keys, when a couple of other smokers came over for a chat.

They were American, but apart from that they were a pleasant enough couple – Bill and MaryJayne from Lawnton near Harrisburg PA (or so they told me). They chatted away and I listened. I missed Ron. Ron could be bloody irritating with his yacking on about web sites and football, but it would have been better that being told all the time what a wonderful country I live in.

They offered to buy me a drink. Things looked up. In fact they bought me a few. Then Pullit came over with the tray of drinks and said, 'there you go, Grandad'.

MaryJayne lit up. 'Hey!' says she 'Are you the guy who writes that *Head Rambles* thing? We love that. It's so funny the way you rise us Americans.'

I admitted I was. I hate that. I like my anonymity. I cursed the odds that had placed them there. With odds like that I should be winning the lottery instead of having my ears bent. They waffled on and on about how amaaazing it was to meet me and all the things I had written and wasn't it a scream how I had invented this joke about shooting tourists.

'It is just a joke, isn't it?' said MaryJayne and went off into shrieks of laughter.

I assured her that it was. I offered them a lift back to their Bed and Breakfast. They accepted. As it happened, it wasn't far from the landfill site.

A CHOICE BETWEEN TWO TERRORISTS

I have a beard. I have had it now for thirty-six years and have no intention of shaving it off. I like it. Herself likes it. And it annoys my sister-in-law (which is enough reason in itself).

For many years I kept it short. That was fine, but people kept saying I looked like Gerry Adams.

I didn't particularly like the comparison and nor, in fairness, did he.

I decided to let it grow a bit. Quite a lot in fact. The problem now is that people say I look like Osama bin Laden.

Why they can't compare me to George Bernard Shaw or someone like that, I don't know. They just insist on comparing me to terrorists. At least I don't look like a tourist! Actually Osama and I have a lot in common. We both like living in the mountains, and we value our privacy. We both have a slight distaste for George W. I must look him up on Facebook, give him a poke and become friends with him.

The beard is getting a bit long now, and I was going to become Gerry Adams again, but a problem has arisen. A few days ago, Puppychild was here. She is a very affectionate child and is inclined to ambush one with a sudden kiss or a cuddle. She sidled up to me and she pointed to my beard.

'That's Grandad,' says she.

Then she gently stroked my beard.

'It's gorgeous,' says she.

What's a bloke to do?

IRELAND IS THE FASTEST COUNTRY IN EUROPE

You may or may not be aware that the pint is safe.

The EU in all its wisdom has decided that the UK and

Ireland may retain our imperial measurements, like the mile and the pound (weight, not money) and the pint.

A couple of years ago, the government spent a fortune metricating our speeds on the roads. All the speed limit signs had to be changed and we were inundated with advertising and little reminder stickers to put on our windscreens. I even got the instruments in my car metricated.

So where do we stand now?

I rang the department yesterday to find out. I eventually got onto a very nice girl, but she seemed a bit upset. I asked her what she was upset about and she told me that she was sitting in the dark, because the new Green minister wouldn't allow them use electricity as it was environmentally unfriendly. So she had no light or computer and hadn't been able to update her Bebo account in weeks. I pointed out she could do that from home, but apparently she can't find her way out of the office, because the minister had had the windows bricked up to save heat and it's so dark in there that she can't find the door. It seems she has been surviving all summer by eating memos and drinking Tippex. But she's bursting to go to the loo.

I asked her what the situation was, now that we are back to driving miles instead of kilometres, and presumably speeding at miles per hour and not kilometres per hour. I asked if they were going to change all the speed signs back again. She said that they still had all the old signs and were keeping them in storage along with the electronic voting machines. However, she said that they wouldn't be replacing them again as it would cost too much and would confuse too many people.

So they have decided we can interpret the signs as we wish. When you see a speed limit sign that says 100, you can interpret that as 100 miles per hour or 100 kilometres per hour.

She said she'd confirm that by email as soon as she could find her way out, and could get to the nearest Internet cafe.

So, in the meantime, I'm heading off for the nearest motorway to see if I can hit 120 miles per hour.

LISTEN HARD TO THE SILENCE

Will someone please explain to me what this iPhone and iPod thing is all about? Surely a phone is a phone and a pod is where you get peas?

Everyone seems to be blogging about them as if they are some great essential to life, like vitamins or tobacco. There are people frantically posting about iPhones and the best one to get and how the one they just got doesn't work.

And I don't understand the craze for iPods at all. I gather that iPods are something to do with listening to music. Why? Why do people have to listen to music all the time? Can people no longer function without some racket going on in their ears? Can people not enjoy the silence of their own thoughts? Or do the kids of today not have thoughts any more?

And iPhones? I gather this has something to do with getting the Internet on your phone? This is crazy! Has modern society become so hooked up on technology that they can't exist without instant access to their emails or the latest news?

If I want the Internet, I fire up my PC. It's great. I can do my shopping, or research the latest disease that Herself thinks she has. I can bore the pants off people by scribbling in my blog. But why would I feel a sudden need to order my groceries while sitting in the bus on the way to work? My emails can wait. They are mostly Cialis, Viagra and penis enlargements.

If I want to listen to music, I'll turn on the radio. If I don't have a radio with me, I'll listen to the sounds around me. I'll think. I'll meditate. I'll ponder the meaning of life. I don't need a constant roar in my ears. The tinnitus takes care of that anyway.

I see ads now urging you to subscribe to services where they will send you the latest news headlines or the latest scores. Is your life so shallow that you are incomplete if you don't know that someone has just scored a goal? Are you going to whither and die because you didn't hear *immediately* that George W. has just waged war against Sweden?

Come on, people! Unhook yourselves from technology and become human beings again.

Unless of course you're reading this post on your Blackberry. In which case, it's all right.

SATISFACTORY TESTS

The Managing Director
Munitions R Us
Harrisburgh
PA
USA

Dear Sir,

I would like to acknowledge receipt of 500 of your Ranger Mk I Anti-SUV Smart Missiles.

We have conducted preliminary tests with these and have found them to be eminently satisfactory.

They were able to distinguish SUVs even on crowded motorways.

In particular, we would like to say how impressed we are with your use of fuel-air explosive. Not only does this vaporise the missile, but also the target vehicle as well, thus leaving no trace of the incident and an intact road surface.

Our R&D department has examined your product and is extremely impressed with the standard of manufacture.

We would suggest one or two minor improvements, however. We have discovered that if you modify integrated chip I377 by short-circuiting legs 34 and 39, and introduce a 5pf capacitor between leg 16 on I29A to chassis, the missile is also capable of seeking out and destroying Jedi. We thought you might like to incorporate this in future production models.

We are currently close to a modification that will seek out and destroy supporters of George W.

We would like to place a preliminary order for a further 1,000 of these missiles to be dispatched forthwith.

Looking forward to doing continuing business with you.

Yours faithfully,
Grandad.

A QUIET MUG OF COFFEE

It was a lovely day on Saturday. I decided to wander down to the village for a coffee and to get some petrol for the mower.

It was beautiful outside the coffee shop. Sandy lay at my feet and went to sleep in the sun. I got chatting to a couple of local blokes who are dog lovers. There were another couple of tourists at the other table. They were both men and were holding hands. I decided to leave them alone because it was a nice day and I don't want to be accused of homophobia.

Now one of the tourists stood up and tripped over Sandy. She didn't mind. But he then turned around and kicked her in the ribs. Sandy minded *that*. Quick as lightning, she jumped to her feet and took his leg off, clean below the knee. She has *very* powerful jaws.

Tourist fell to the ground (he hadn't much option) and my two pals started lacing into him, as we hate cruelty to animals. Tourist's boyfriend started having hysterics and he started throwing things at me. He threw a plate. It missed.

It bounced off the windscreen of an SUV that was driving past. The driver was a Yummy Mummy who was yacking on her mobile phone at the time so whatever concentration she had left was gone, and she drove into the back of a tourist bus, and exploded in a ball of flame. Well, I'm not sure if it was herself or the SUV that exploded, but it was quite spectacular.

People started running around throwing jugs of water and milk on the SUV. I had my 10 litres of petrol that I'd bought for the lawnmower, and someone grabbed it and threw that on the conflagration. That didn't help.

In the meantime, tourist's boyfriend was really beginning to annoy me, screeching at me and throwing bread rolls at me, so I kicked him in the nuts. That shut him up. The other bloke was pumping blood on the ground and managed to mutter something about suing me. I couldn't resist it. I told him he hadn't a leg to stand on.

We went home then. There was no point in staying because the peace and tranquillity of the moment was gone. I let Sandy keep the leg as a souvenir.

Bloody tourists.

PUT THAT FINGER THERE AND WE WILL NEVER SPEAK AGAIN

I went to see the doctor yesterday.

'Howya, Doc,' says I.

'Howya, Grandad. Are ya well?' says he, which is a weird question from a doctor. Is he hoping that I am, or that I'm not?

'Grand,' says I, 'just here for the 10,000 mile service.'

So he poked me and prodded me and we talked about this and that. He listened to various parts of me, but not what I was saying. I'm used to that. Blood pressure – normal. Heart – normal. Lungs – normal (Yup! I can carry on puffing away). Teeth – none. Hearing – brilliant (apart from the tinnitus). All in all, he reckons I'm good for a few miles yet.

Then he put on a rubber glove and started talking about prostates. Jayzus! I was across the floor and standing splayed with my back to the wall before I knew it. I'm not having anyone poking around there. There are limits to my friendships. How can you greet a bloke in the village when he's had his finger up your arse?

'Relax,' says he, 'I'm just going to take some blood.'

He did. About a gallon. It left me feeling quite drained, but I don't mind.

He asked me then about the tourist shooting, and how it was going. It transpired that he wanted to join up. This was great news as this means that the only non-member in the village now is the gravedigger. He's too busy to join.

'What about the Hippocratic Oath?' says I.

We pondered this for a few minutes, but we decided it only applied to patients. And by definition, a tourist isn't a patient. So I signed him up. We're going hunting next week. But I'm going to make damn sure he is some distance away from me when I go squatting in the undergrowth.

A CHANGE IN VOTING PATTERNS

The doorbell rang a few minutes ago. I went to see who it was. A very nice young couple with clipboards, who are updating the Electoral Register.

Now most of the people around here are away or out, and I was one of the few people they found actually in residence. I put on my most trustworthy, 'Grandad knows best' face and told them not to worry, that I'd update them on all the people around here. They were very relieved, because it was raining and would save them a lot of knocking on doors.

So we sat down and went through the list. I had to make a few changes for them, because there has been a lot of coming and going since they last made the list.

I now have an extra five sons, and four daughters living at home and all of voting age. My next-door neighbour is now Micheál Loch and the house across the lane is owned by Finn and Mary McCool. I told them that the people in the thatched house had moved to Spain on a permanent basis (unless of course the warrant is quashed on appeal). I said that the new owners depended on the Criminal Assets Bureau, who had seized the property.

It should be interesting, come the next election. And between Herself and myself, we have an extra nine votes.

HOW TO GET RID OF A WASPS' NEST

For some strange reason a lot of people visit my site because they are trying to get rid of wasps. I'm not really an expert on this subject.

The only wasps' nest I ever got rid of was in the neighbour's eaves. That was simple. Though I did overdo the petrol a bit, and they are still rebuilding the house. The wasps are gone though.

Last year, I had a great holiday in France. We stayed in a wee gîte in the middle of nowhere in the Lot region. It was beautiful there. The scenery was fantastic, and the weather was almost too hot. There was a patio out the back, where we used to sit until well after dark.

The only problem we had there was wasps. They were fucking huge. I'm talking about the 747s of the wasp world here. There was a fig tree by the patio and they loved that, so there were always plenty around.

So I got myself a fly swatter or two and I practised my John McEnroe serve. I became damn good at it. I'd wait until one was flying over me and then do my serve. If I missed, then they ignored me, but if I hit one then there would be a lovely crisp smack and another wasp would head to hornet heaven.

My ace was to hit one good and square. He'd go sailing across the lane into the long grass on the other side, whereupon there would be an explosion of startled crickets. Quite a spectacular site! By the end of the holiday, I was ready to sign up for Wimbledon.

LIVING CAN BE FATAL

I watched a programme last night on television. It was about the NHS in the UK. They have come up with a rather neat way of saving money. They will only operate on you if they approve of your lifestyle. The programme gave quite a few examples.

There was the woman who had an arthritic hip joint which had totally collapsed. As a result of this, she couldn't walk. As a result of her immobility, she put on a few pounds. So they wouldn't operate on her as she was 'obese' (she weighed a little more than me). They told her to lose a few pounds by exercising! She had to go abroad in the end.

There was another man who needed an operation on his leg. They wouldn't operate on him because he smoked. His smoking had nothing to do with his operation. They just didn't like the fact that he smoked.

There was another case of a man who needed a triple bypass. He also smoked, so they refused. You might say that there was cause here, but the surgeon made it quite plain that he would do the operation, no problem, if the man went private. That man died shortly after.

So why do they operate on footballers and rugby players? Surely these people are going to go out and injure themselves again? They have unhealthy lifestyles. Why do they fix skiers' broken legs?

This could be extended indefinitely.

They will probably in the future refuse to operate on people with driving licences. They're only going to go out and have another smash. Or people who drink? Or children?

Or people who will insist on going outdoors? Or anyone who has any DIY equipment in their houses? How about people who eat? They are surely going to rush out after an operation and become obese?

This could really catch on. Mary Harney take note.

ARE YOU A BUM PUFFER?

A couple of weeks ago, I got chatting to a bloke. He asked me if I was a Bum Puffer.

To cut a long story short, he's making good progress. He can now feed through a tube through what's left of his jaw. They managed to remove his right leg from his rectum and sew it back on. And they are hopeful that they will find his arms somewhere.

But this got me thinking. What exactly is a Bum Puffer? I did a search on the Interweb and came up with nothing. I even tried the urban slang sites. I tried gay sites. Not a mention. I tried sites about flatulence. Rien. Nada.

Then a nice chap contacted me from Australia. He explained. Apparently Bum Puffing is the act of smoking without inhaling. That's all. Trust the Australians to make something simple sound crude.

So I *am* a Bum Puffer. I'm Bum Puffing as I write.

I feel bad now. I suppose I had better visit that bloke and apologise. I'll bring him some grapes. I'll liquidise them first.

TRAINING FOR ASSASSINATION

I decided yesterday to visit the 'bum puffer' bloke in hospital.

I drove over the mountains to the coast, and caught the train. It was only when I got on the train, and the doors were firmly shut that the driver cheerily announced that I was on the express to Maynooth. I like the way they do that – they give you the destinations *after* the doors are shut and the train is moving. So you can't change your mind. I suppose it's one way of getting people to see the country? Luckily it stopped at the station I was going to, anyway.

The hospital had changed beyond all recognition since the last time I was there. That was the day I left RTÉ. I first entered RTÉ in 1971, on a Yamaha 90cc motorbike, and I left in 2001 in an ambulance. But that's another story.

I saw the patient. They had done quite a good job on him. The only mistake they made was to sew back his arms the wrong way around, so if he decides to take up the piano, it will be interesting.

On the way back, I just knew it was going to happen. Men have intuition too. I knew I was going to meet my old pal Raymond, who I haven't seen in years. So I strolled into the station and there he was. He was leaning on the wall, staring into the distance, and smoking his pipe. So I leaned against the wall beside him and smoked mine.

'Howya, Raymond,' says I.

'Jayzus! Grandad! What are you doing here?' says he.

So we leaned against the wall and talked about old times.

Trains came and went, but it was pleasant there in the sunshine. It turns out he has been stalking an old arch-enemy of mine. He wants to kill him and so do I. So eventually we caught our train and made our plans on the way home.

It was a good day. I met an old friend, and I'm going to enjoy working with Raymond. And I got the €5 back off that bloke in the hospital that I had loaned him.

Which was the reason I visited in the first place.

RAMBLES IN THE HILLS

A couple of days ago, the doctor and I went hunting. As a new member of the club, I wanted him to have a good day. And it was. It was a glorious day. It was one of those crisp autumn afternoons, when the birds sang and the sun shone.

We were sitting on a rock, quietly enjoying the scent of the heather and bracken when a buck deer appeared. He was a magnificent specimen. He looked at us in that regal manner that only a buck can conjure. Like lightning, Doc had his rifle up and sighted. He snapped off a quick shot. It was amazing to see the speed of his reaction.

It was a beautiful kill. One shot, straight through the temple. We went down to examine the body. It was a German tourist who had been just about to shoot the deer. Bastard! I hate people who kill for pleasure. We left him there for the foxes. I think Doc is going to be a good addition to the club.

We were heading back, and he told me some of my blood test results were back. He apologised for mixing business with pleasure, but I said that was OK.

Apparently, I have a deficiency in my alcohol levels, and my nicotine count is alarmingly low. He gave me two prescriptions there and then. One is for three pints of Guinness to be taken nightly and the other is for 25 grams of pipe tobacco to be taken daily as required. These can be dispensed at the local pub and the tobacconist, in case the chemist is closed. And they are both covered by the Drug Refund Scheme. So it won't cost me anything.

When you get older, it is vital to have a good doctor.

GOD TO SUE AMERICA

In an unprecedented move, God is to sue America under international anti-trust and copyright legislation.

Head Rambles contacted the Heaven press office and arranged an interview with their spokesangel Gabriel.

HR: Thank you for speaking to us Gay. Can you tell us what this is all about?

G: You're welcome, Grandad. Yes. This move was taken because God has decided that enough is enough and the use of His name has to be protected.

HR: But I thought anyone is free to use the name of God?

G: Yes. But there are limits. America has breached the anti-trust legislation by claiming God as their own to the exclusion of all others.

HR: Can you elaborate?

G: Where do I start? The American insistence that they are 'God's own country'? Their everyday naming of God in their war-promoting anthem? The constant 'God bless America'? They even have His name on their currency, which is a bit ironic considering His son's attitude to moneylenders in the temple. He is sick and tired of it. The final straw came when that idiot leader of theirs started to claim he was starting wars because God told him to.

HR: But doesn't every country claim that God is on their side?

G: Yes. But the Americans do it to extreme. They have breached copyright by appropriating God for themselves.

HR: Have you sought the opinion of the Pope on this matter?

G: Who?

HR: The Pope? The bloke in the Vatican?

G: Oh, him. He has nothing to do with us. You are confusing faith and religion. A common mistake. God gave you faith. You invented religion for yourselves. That has nothing to do with God.

HR: Do you not think this is a bit unfair? I mean God could have given them some indication that He was not happy with the situation.

G: Don't make me laugh. They have had enough warnings. Mount Saint Helens volcano? Tornados? Hurricanes? The Oakland's earthquake? Drought? Floods? Blizzards? Hailstorms? What more do they want? San Francisco is next to go.

HR: But lots of counties suffer these disasters.

G: True. But how many countries suffer from *all* of them? That should have given the Americans a hint. We even concentrated on their so call 'Bible Belt' but they still wouldn't shut up. If anything, it made them worse.

HR: But other people commit atrocities in the name of religion?

G: Here you go with the 'religion' thing again. That has nothing to do with us.

HR: What do you think your chances are of success?

G: We know the outcome. We will win. Don't forget, we can see the future.

HR: Well, thank you for your time, Gay. You have been very candid.

G: My pleasure, Grandad. You know God is a great fan of yours? You are on the top of His Feed Reader.

HR: Wow! I'm honoured. One last question though?

G: Fire away.

HR: How does God intend to take the oath if He is called to give evidence?

G: Good question! We're still working on that one.

HOW NOT TO LOOK LIKE A TOURIST

Ireland is a nice country to visit. The people are friendly and the Guinness is good.

I realise however, that I might have put some of you off with my tales of tourist shooting (one of our national sports). So, just for you nice people who read my blatherings, I'm going to give some pointers on 'How not to look like a tourist'. This could save your life, so read carefully.

Dress appropriately

Irish people do not wear shorts, unless on the beach. Nor do they wear coats, unless it's pissing out of the heavens. Loud colours are frowned upon, unless you are female or have female inclinations. The general rule is dress scruffy. A dab of cow-shit on the footwear is also good. Irish people never, ever, wear Aran Sweaters. These were invented purely for ripping off Americans, and are a dead giveaway.

Travelling

Never stop to read a road sign. All Irish people know that Irish road signs point in the wrong direction anyway and ignore them. Anyone examining a road sign is a tourist by definition.

Never ask for directions. You will more than likely end up over a cliff, or up in the bogs. If you are really lost, then be cunning. If you want to find the way to (say) Killarney, then stop someone and say, 'Jayzus, I need to be at a wedding in Killarney and I'm running late. What's the quickest way?'

If you have non-Irish registration plates on your car, remove them. If you feel naked without them, then rob an Irish set off a parked car. You must also learn to drive like the Irish. Never indicate. Always hog the overtaking lane. Always drive too fast. Never take a bend on the correct side of the road. Always drive like you have just drunk a bottle of whiskey. Actually, to be on the safe side, it's probably better to drink a bottle of whiskey before venturing anywhere.

Communicating

This is a tricky one. An accent is a complete giveaway. Though with the current influx of immigrants, you are a bit safer. American accents are still not tolerated, so Americans should not speak at all. And if you must speak, keep your voices down. For some reason, tourists are always the noisiest table in the pub. Or anywhere else, for that matter.

If you come across a nice view, or something scenic, then, for God's sake, just grunt. Loud exclamations of appreciation or telling Harry to get the video camera are out.

That's enough for now.

COMPUTERS ARE A CURSE

It's the same damned story every morning. I switch on my laptop.
Me: Mornin' laptop. Ready for some work?
Laptop: Hold on. I'm still loading.

I wait a while.
Me: Are you ready yet?
Laptop: Fire away.

I try to load my mail thing.

Laptop: Hold on. I'm checking for updates for your anti-virus.

I play Solitaire for a while.
Me: OK now?
Laptop: Yup.

I check my mail. Nothing happens.
Me: What's wrong now?
Laptop: There are some software updates for you. I'm downloading them.

Back to the Solitaire.
Laptop: OK. All downloaded and installed. You have to reboot now.
Me: Fuck off. I'm not going through all this again.
Laptop: Fair enough, but you have been warned.

I check my mail. Nothing there except the usual penis enhancers and Fred wanting me to write to her for nude photos. I fire up my browser. Nothing happens.
Me: What are you at now?
Laptop: Just scanning your disk for nasty stuff. Shouldn't take more than an hour.

I'm bored with Solitaire, so I switch to Minesweeper. Eventually, I get my browser running and I do my little bit of surfing.
Laptop: You really ought to reboot, you know?
Me: I told you. No fucking way!

Laptop: You're playing with fire.

I ignore it and start on the wittiest post for my blog that I have thought up in ages. It takes a long time to write.
Laptop: Alert! Virus found in F drive!
Me: Fuck off. I don't have an F drive. You're only doing this to wind me up.
Laptop: True.

I'm nearly finished.
Laptop: You forgot to switch on at the mains and your battery has run out. Byeeeee!

plop

CHRISTMAS IS OVER AT LAST

I was down in the pub on Saturday. The local shopkeepers were having their monthly meeting in the corner of the bar.

Why is it that a lot of thing that happen on a monthly basis seem to involve a lot of bad temper, shouting and general irrational behaviour?

We usually ignore them, because they discuss things like speed bumps and litterbins, and nothing ever gets done anyway. They all seem to hate each other and every meeting ends in a fight, which can be fun to watch.

On Saturday, they were discussing the Christmas decorations for the village. They used to keep the decorations in the local police station, but they were stolen from there, so now they take it in turns to store them when they're not in use. A row broke out as to who was storing them this year. They all denied having them. The row turned ugly. It went from the usual shouting and name-calling through to a full-blown pitched battle. Soon the glasses were flying and fists swinging. It was great craic.

It began to get really ugly when the bar stools started flying, so I thought I'd better step in. I threw a full pint through the television screen, which made a spectacular bang. It was a waste of a good pint, but it stopped the fight.

Gráinne, who runs the local hairdressers came over. She was dripping all over the place because the butcher had just shoved her head down the toilet and flushed it.

'What did you do that for?' she snarled.

'I know where your decorations are,' I replied.

She looked at me open-mouthed and dripped a bit more. Not a pretty sight.

'You never took them down after last Christmas. They're still up there,' I said.

There was a silence for a moment (apart from the television which was still fizzling and crackling on its shelf). Then they all rushed for the door. They quietly came back in and admitted I was right.

So they spent yesterday taking all the decorations down. They had to do that because they had hired someone to put them up again today. Who says village life is dull?

LINUX IS A LOAD OF BILLUX

I woke early this morning.

I thought as I had some time to spare I'd try putting Linux on my PC. I had already copied down the file from the Interweb, so I put it on a floppy and stuck it in my floppy drive. (No jokes please). I rebooted.

It made some funny noises, but things seemed to go all right. But then it started asking me questions. It wanted to know where to put the Linux and did I want to use my whole hard drive?

I have my faithful crappy copy of Windows on the PC that works most of the time, and I didn't want to lose that. Or my collection of ~~porn~~ photographs. So I had to switch the PC off and start again.

This time I went into Windows and cleared up some space. Then I went back to my Linux again.

All went well. I found the space and I told Linux it could do what it wanted with that, and it seemed happy. I went off to make my fifth mug of tea.

I came back to find it was complaining about my hard disk. It said it was faulty. Bollox. It's only ten years old, so it can't be that bad. And the little pop-up thingy that was complaining wouldn't go away.

So I had to start again from scratch. This time it worked. Everything went in. It told me to reboot, which I did. It looks nice. Uncluttered. Clean. Nice colours.

I told it to connect to the Interweb, but it refused. So I had to try to find out what was wrong. And I ended up going around and around in circles. I eventually got it connected after another six mugs of tea.

So I started browsing the Interweb. No problem. Of course everything looked the same as it did in Windows, only much slower.

I went to see what else was there. Nothing. None of the programmes I need are around, except for a text editor and a copy of Open Office. I opened that and tried to read some of my old documents, but it's confusing. I'm used to my old ways. I'm too old to change.

I did find some games. Linux provides a lot more games than Windows. But that's a lot of trouble to go to just to play a game. In the end, I went back to Windows. Windows may not work, but at least I know where all the programmes that don't work, are.

Time for another mug of tea.

YESTERDAY WAS FRIDAY AND TOMORROW IS MONDAY

Most of the time I know what I am doing. Most of the time I know where I am. Rarely do I know *when* I am.

This seems to be a problem in this household. We keep getting confused as to what day of the week it is. In fact, I had to buy a watch especially. I like analogue watches, because I have always used them. I hate digital watches. So I have an analogue watch with a digital display on it that shows me the date, and more importantly the day.

Yesterday, I received an email from one of my probation

officers. He wanted a report (for the courts or something) and he wanted it urgently. I wrote back and said I was busy (because you can't let these people boss you around). I said I would do it over the weekend and would have it for him by Monday. Then I realised that it was Tuesday and not Friday, and I had to write back and apologise. And I hate apologising to probation officers. It upsets the natural pecking order.

With one thing and another, things are a bit hectic here at the moment. Gone are the glory days when I could relax and surf around the blogs, not leaving comments on them (yes – I'm a lurker). Gone are the days where I could have a reply for everyone who commented.

You see, I suddenly have a whole load of things to do on the work front and it is annoying me. My ~~punters~~ clients keep changing the goal posts and they suddenly want everything yesterday (having been quite happy and quiet for most of the year).

All I want to do now is take a nap. But I can't because I have so much to do.

So if I'm a bit erratic with my writing in the future, I'm sorry. I'm tired. I'm weary. God help me if the battery in my watch dies.

SMOKING IS GOOD FOR YOU

Whenever there is a survey about health, they invariably ask if you smoke. Then they ask how many cigarettes a day. But they never mention a pipe. And I often wondered how pipe smoking equated to cigarette smoking. I meant to ask the doctor. And then it struck me – why not look it up on the Interweb?

So I did. And what I found surprised even me. It has been suggested that a pipe-smoker who smokes up to four bowlfuls of tobacco a day can have a longer life expectancy than someone who doesn't smoke at all.

Of course the anti-smoking Nazis would have us believe that even *thinking* about tobacco is enough to bring on a brain tumour, so the idea of smoking prolonging life is pure heresy. So how can the pipe be healthy, if tobacco is so evil? Simple. The key to the whole issue lies in stress.

When calculating a person's expected lifespan, there are many factors to consider – heredity, lifestyle, general health and mental well-being. Of these, mental well-being is considered to be one of the greatest factors. Being happy and relaxed in you life is enough to add years onto your life expectancy. Relaxation is the key. Stress is the killer.

To me, every aspect of cigarette smoking screams of stress – frantically jamming the fag in the mouth, the rapid dragging on it and the final stabbing of the cigarette in the ashtray. Pipe smoking is a ritual. By its nature, it's a relaxing process – the careful packing of the tobacco into the pipe, the ritual of lighting it (a quick stab of a lighter isn't good enough here) and then sitting back and enjoying it. I even find the process of cleaning a pipe relaxing. People even say that the sight of another person smoking a pipe is relaxing.

People accuse me of inventing the stuff I write about. I'm very hurt by that, but I'll let it pass. I will take my information from the Surgeon General of the United States in his 1964 report on the dangers of tobacco.

Specifically, this report confirmed that cigarette smoking could be dangerous, but noted that the results of several studies about pipe smokers showed they tended to live longer than the general population!

So. Throw away those damned cigarettes. They stink and they are dangerous. Put it in your pipe and smoke it.

I WILL HAVE TO GRINDLE LINUX

Since I installed Linux the other day, I have been regretting it. I have a habit of switching on the PC and then going off and making a mug of tea. Now when I come back, the fucking thing is running Linux and I want it to run Windows. So I have to reboot every time and wait for a menu to pop up. I then have about .0035 of a second to scroll down and select Windows.

That pisses me off.

So I did a bit of research. Apparently there is a thing called lilo. We used to have one of those for lying on the beach. There is a file called etc/lilo.conf which I have to change. So I went looking for it. No sign of it!

I did more research.

The Linux I installed is called Ubuntu and it uses a thing called Grub. Where the fuck do they get these names? They have the most obscure names for everything. You don't 'search' or 'find' – you 'grep'. And the desktop is called 'Gnome' or 'KDE'.

I found the grub file and it wasn't where it was supposed to be. It had been laid somewhere else. I opened it in Kate (I rest my case!) and found a block of lines that mentioned Windows. They were at the bottom, so I moved them to the top.

I went to save the file, and it wouldn't let me. It said I didn't have permission! *My* computer that *I* bought with *my* money has the neck to tell me I don't have permission!

I have reared a child. I know about authority. So I told it in no uncertain terms, that if it didn't let me write the file, it was going to be grounded for a month, and that I'd stick burnt matches in its USB ports and use the CD tray as a pipe rack. It relented.

It let me write the file and it now starts up properly. I should think so too. Fucking little upstart!

DANIEL O'DONNELL HAS HIS USES

Me: Why do you do that?
Laptop: Why do I do what?
Me: Every now and then you spin your hard disk and then flip open the CD drive.
Laptop: Because I can.
Me: Stop it. It's annoying me.
Laptop: Oh, shut up and stop whining. Go back to your pathetic blogging.
Me: If you do it once more, I shall get really annoyed.

Laptop: Tough shit.

click

Laptop: Aaaahhhh! Get that fucking Daniel O'Donnell audio disk out of there!

Me: Do you promise to behave?

Laptop: Yes! Yes! Anything!! Just take it away. Bastard!

heh

IT WAS A DARK AND WINDY NIGHT

There was a loud knock on the door last night. We don't get many kids coming around here at Hallowe'en because they have learned their lesson in the past. So I was a bit surprised.

I opened the door, and there was a very tall figure there. He was taller than me, and I'm over six foot. He was dressed all in black with a hood over his face. I hate hoodies.

'What the fuck do you want?' says I.

'I have come for you,' he said. He had a strange voice. It echoed around inside my head and made me feel uncomfortable.

'You can piss off,' says I. 'You interrupted me in the middle of a good book and I'm not going anywhere!'

'Who is it?' yells Herself from the kitchen.

'Some tosser looking for apples, or something.'

'Tell him to piss off.'

'I did, but he's still here.'

Herself came shooting out of the kitchen, frying pan in hand. It never ceases to amaze me how fast she can move when she has the bile up. She shot out the door. There was a loud clang and a louder yell. I nearly felt sorry for him.

'Is he gone?' says I.

'I don't know,' says Herself. 'He just sort of crumpled on the ground. I think I killed him.'

'Fair play,' says I, 'I'll get the lamp.'

We went out by lamplight and there was the cloak on the ground. No sign of the bloke, which was strange. Even stranger, there was an old scythe lying beside the cloak. I took it inside. It was very old, but with a bit of cleaning it should be OK. It will come in handy next summer when the grass starts growing again.

'I love it when you're angry,' says I to Herself.

She gave me a dirty look and went back into the kitchen.

I'VE GOT YOU UNDER MY SKIN

Yesterday started off as a good day. My mood was good, and what was even better, we had finally shifted the worst of the weather over to America. It was cold, but the sun was shining. We decided to go down to the village.

Everything changed.

As soon as we arrived in the village, the mood took a downer. Bing Crosby was singing Christmas melodies *very* loudly throughout the place. I hate Bing Crosby. Well, I don't hate Bing Crosby himself, as I don't know him, but I hate his singing. And that goes for Sinatra and all that lot as well. The sound of *White Christmas* and all that shite really gets under my skin, so I could feel the kill instinct coming to the fore.

I decided to calm myself with a mug of coffee while Herself went shopping. Sandy and I wandered over to the coffee shop, where there were a few people sitting out, supping their coffee and giving out stink about Crosby.

Then I saw them. The best tables nearest the heater had 'No Smoking' signs on them. And this was *outside* in the open fucking air! I complained very loudly to the owner. She agreed with me, because she likes a smoke or two herself, but said the health inspector had insisted.

Who are these fucking Nazis? They have driven us outside and are still complaining.

At this stage, I was spitting venom and was getting near what my psychiatrist calls 'explosion point'. I set fire to the 'no smoking signs'. In fairness to them, they didn't make much smoke.

One of the customers complained when I burned the sign on his table. He made a *LOT* of smoke.

WILL IT LAST UNTIL 2067?

By now you must all think I hate Christmas. I don't. What I hate is the modern Christmas.

When I was a lad, back in the 1950s, Christmas was a

very special occasion. We looked forward to it with great anticipation, and counted down the days. I remember the excitement of bringing out the advent calendar and opening the windows on it each day. It made Christmas seem nearer.

There was never any sign of Christmas coming in those days. The big shops in Dublin used to put up lights and I remember taking trips into the city just to see the lights on McBernies on the Quays (I think they were called McBernies. Does anyone remember?). But there was never a sign of trees or decorations anywhere else.

Christmas Eve was the start. On that day, we used to buy the tree. There was huge excitement and we'd spend the afternoon putting it up and decorating it. Some households even waited until the children were in bed and asleep before putting the tree up.

So Christmas morning was a time of great excitement. We would wake at about four. First of all we'd dive for our stockings at the foot of the bed. These held lovely little things. A tube of sweets and little toys (all very inexpensive but that never bothered us in the slightest). Of course there was an apple and an orange too. We would play with these until the grown-ups were up and about.

The day had come, the house was decorated and the tree was up, shining in the corner. After mass, we'd have a big family opening of presents. The presents were rarely big, but they were so special. There were games, jigsaws, Dinky toys and all sorts of things. None of them needed batteries, just imagination. We would play with them all day, apart from the mealtimes.

I still have quite a few of those Dinky cars and Matchbox

cars. When Puppychild visits, she always plays with them. She loves them. They have lasted nearly sixty years.

Christmas lasted for twelve days. On Epiphany (6 January), the tree and the decorations would be taken down and we'd start looking forward to spring.

Nowadays, it is all so different.

I am sick of the mention of Christmas by mid November. Every fucking advertisement on television is telling me that my Christmas won't be perfect unless I have a new suite of furniture, or a new phone, or some stinking scent or other. Every shop I enter is playing tacky Christmas music at me. Houses are lit up like Heathrow airport for weeks in advance. When Christmas Day arrives, it is no different from any of the preceding fifty days.

The 'gifts' children get are ridiculous. They don't get anything special because they belong to the 'I want it NOW' generation, so they already have everything. So the poor parents have to get a second mortgage, or tap the moneylender to buy a Wii or a flat screen TV for the children's room.

Of course the presents the children get are not what they want. They are the presents that the television tells them they want, or their friends. Peer pressure is the key these days. All the toys have to have batteries and remote controls. The dolls speak and walk and dance. The children need no imagination whatsoever. They are bored with the things after a couple of days (if the yokes haven't broken in the meantime).

So here is a question. Of all the toys that will be given this Christmas, how many will still be giving magic and fun in sixty years time?

LINUX OR WINDOWS?

Me: Mornin'.
Laptop: Whatever.
Me: Have you finished all that crap with downloading stuff and checking things?
Laptop: Maybe. Maybe not.
Me: I've been thinking about this Linux thing. People seem to think it's a good idea.
Laptop: Fucking nerdheads. What would those wankers know?
Me: There is no need for that language. I want to give it a try anyway.
Laptop: You want me to switch?
Me: OK. Let's go for it.
Laptop: >>>>>> reboot
Me: kjjsu ^hdh lk kjudfg?
Laptop: Try a different text editor.
Me: Got it. This seems fine. Yup. I've found the Internet.
Laptop: Big fucking deal.
Me: I can't find PhotoShop.
Laptop: You don't have PhotoShop on Linux. You'll have to use Gimp.
Me: I don't know Gimp! How long will it take me to learn?
Laptop: That and all the other different programmes? A looooong time. *heh*
Me: This is no good. I have stuff that has to be done today. Go back to Windows.

Laptop: Tosser! +++++ & reboot.
Me: That's better.
Laptop: Critical error! NTFS partition failed. Contact Microsoft immediately. System files corrupt or missing. System shutdown! System shutdown! Pffffffff …

sigh